# The New
# Older Woman

# The New Older Woman

## A Dialogue for the Coming Century

Peggy Downes, Ph.D.
Patricia Faul
Virginia Mudd
Ilene Tuttle

CELESTIAL ARTS
*Berkeley, California*

Celestial Arts Publishing
P.O. Box 7123
Berkeley, California 94707

Cover design: Fifth Street
Interior design and typesetting: Star Type

Printed in the United States of America

Library of Congress Card Number
95-72323

First Printing, 1996
1 2 3 4 / 99 98 97 96

# Contents

# Foreword

*by Gail Sheehy*

It was early 1991. The invitation intrigued me: a five-day dialogue with ten older American women at Esalen Institute, a spa/retreat on California's Big Sur coast. I'd heard of the place, but not the four women who called themselves Group 4. They were asking "women of achievement country-wide from varying professional disciplines" to come talk about being vital, productive and over fifty in today's society. The conference would be called "The New Older Woman."

I was drawn by the concept and the prospect of meeting articulate women who had been through the ups and downs of early and mid-life and who were now facing passages for which we had no names, never mind maps. Even more appealing was the idea that no papers or speeches were requested—just "come and share your thoughts." I packed my duffel and decided to take a chance on the vision Group 4 painted of comfortable, unhurried "interchange" played against a background of hot baths, redwoods and rocky shores. It shouted *California* to my East Coast ears. It was, and more.

At the time, I was working on a book about menopause that would be called *The Silent Passage*. And I was wrestling with a sequel to *Passages*. Research had already astonished me with certain facts:

• A woman who reaches age 50 today—and remains free of cancer and heart disease—can expect to see her 92nd birthday.

• Women passing 50 today, in my national surveys, see themselves entering an "optimistic, can-do" stage of life. Studies show women continue to gain in psychological maturity well into their *60s and 70s.*

In the space of a single generation, since the publication of *Passages* in 1976, we had broken the evolutionary code. I felt like we were on the brink of an astonishing discovery: there is a revolution in the adult life cycle. When our parents turned 50, we thought they were old. Women and men I had been interviewing routinely believed they are five to ten years younger than their birth certificates—and they are.

> 50 is what 40 used to be.
> 60 is what 50 used to be.

As I would later write in *New Passages: Mapping Your Life Across Time,* "People are taking longer to grow up and much longer to die. That shifts all the stages of adulthood ahead— by up to ten years."

I was just beginning to formulate my own concept of a Second Adulthood beginning in middle life. The women assembled by the visionaries of Group 4 were the living proof it existed! Each one was preparing consciously to re-shape a "new self" to give this Second Adulthood its own meaning. But they were way ahead of the curve.

Our conference could be called an intimate '60s-style encounter group; yet, despite the many personal talkathons we had all endured over the years, none of us had ever gathered to talk about being an *older woman.* The participants were savvy and spicy, aged 50 to 80, and we bonded quickly. I was introduced, for the first time, to Catherine Bateson whose mother, Dr. Margaret Mead, had been an inspiring mentor in my professional growth. Catherine, a writer and professor of anthropology at George Mason University in Fairfax, Virginia, was now passing on her own informed views of societal change to a new generation. Each participant added a bold stroke to Group 4's palette: all had made a mark, broken a barrier, made a difference. The wellspring of assembled knowledge and experience spilled out over five days in a seamless flow of candor.

Rather quickly, we hit on something really profound: the source of continuing aliveness is to identify your love and pursue it. Once you have engaged in a creative interplay of yourself in the world, no one can take it away from you. No human associations that may change or fall apart can damage that. It becomes the throughline that makes your life vital and keeps your mind quick, and bridges the discontinuities as loved ones die off. Your passion, once you find it, is always there to provide enrichment and purpose.

Conversations occasionally bordering on "girl-talk" shifted suddenly to intensely passionate accounts. We listened carefully, comfortably together. The air was charged with the strength of women who had faced choices squarely and were now mapping their own way through uncharted territory. As a group, we didn't represent the whole social spectrum. Ours was a narrow socio-economic spread, and we were all aware of the voices missing. But we were a good mix of pacesetters to *begin* a dialogue about how women build the courage to take new steps—and preserve the sense of aliveness. Our views would be a quick sketch for further delineation.

The four dynamic women who put this all together considered themselves inquirers seeking a new direction for themselves. But they had also scored a hit. It became obvious before the week was out that the New Older Woman was a savvy, serene, and sexy new prototype.

We asked Group 4 what they would do with the armload of taped sessions—with their "picture" when the paint dried, the easel folded. As a start in spreading the word, they advised that each of us was free to use conference data for professional writing with permission of the participants quoted. I, for one, have drawn on the dialogues for *The Silent Passage*, published shortly after the Esalen meeting, and more recently, *New Passages: Mapping Your Life Across Time*.

Our question to Group 4 was answered a year later, when, with renewed confidence and vigor, they went on to sponsor a second successful gathering of eleven distinguished women. Their conference report attracted the interest of a publisher and this book became further fruit of the Esalen dialogues. Something tells me it won't be the final word from this foursome.

I join all conference participants in applauding Group 4—Peggy, Pat, Virginia and Ilene—for their curiosity and pizazz in bringing women this "dialogue for the coming century"—a provocative signpost for the passages ahead.

GAIL SHEEHY
*May 15, 1995*

# Introduction

Our joint venture began in a spirit of self-interest in 1990. As four over-sixty women, friends and neighbors for more than half that time, we knew what we *didn't* want from our lives at our age: we *didn't* seek the placid existence that society said we were entitled to or that our senior status implied we deserved. We weren't ready to wind down, or to be more cautious and less adventurous. We were each seeking new challenges, and we decided to join forces, believing that together we could reach higher and look further than we could singly. A month later we took the first step in giving our joint commitment a physical reality—a room, so to speak, of our own.

The office on Monterey's Cannery Row cost $300 a month but had a $3 million view of the boat harbor and a wide-angle shot of the bay's northward-curving shoreline. In a run-down converted cannery, the place's seedy ambiance owed its unique look to a succession of tenants who left recycled barn wood walls, gilt mirrors, and a once-elegant custom carpet embossed with a fading corporate crest. We loved it at first sight and signed the lease, calling ourselves Group 4 for lack of a more seductive title. Though our association still lacked definition, we knew as we surveyed our funky new digs that neither the bizarre decor nor the scenic view matched the elation of having a work space all our own.

The fact that we didn't fit the profile of start-up entrepreneurs, or that we lacked a passionate, well-defined goal, was no bar to our optimism. Our strength was rooted in a common yearning to embark on something new, something productive that would tap into our experience and talents. We had strict criteria: the venture should be challenging, stimulating, and extend beyond our community to a broader constituency; it should not demand eight-hour work days, require a large capital investment, or lose money. What had begun as a personal need for each of us culminated in the formation of our "company." We are:

**PEGGY DOWNES**, Ph.D., sixty-five, married with two children and four step-children, graduate of Vassar College with a BA in Political Science. She is a professor at Santa Clara University, where she has been teaching American politics since earning her doctorate in political science from Claremont Graduate School of Public Policy. While designing pilot courses on the Politics of Aging and Intergenerational Politics for the university, she found an intriguing niche where politics, gerontology, and her work with re-entry women intersected, and she was eager to explore this new academic subject. When Group 4 was formed, Peggy's husband, a former private school headmaster and an educational consultant, was seriously ill. At the time she was seeking a comfortable balance between teaching, research, and caregiving.

**PATRICIA FAUL**, sixty-nine, had just retired from a thirty-year career as an elementary school teacher, and was planning to expand her association with *Earthwatch*, an international program of university research projects. She was also co-authoring a book for pre-adolescents. Pat earned her Bachelor's degree from the University of California,

Berkeley; she has been married for forty-five years to a now-retired college president, and has two adult children. With a long record of community service, she is in her fourth elected term on the board of directors for the local airport, a forum where she interacts comfortably on an all-male turf. Pat felt she needed something like Group 4 to encourage her to pursue writing and teaching, and also to share viewpoints. She particularly wanted a work space separate from her home.

**VIRGINIA MUDD**, sixty-seven, was ready to venture away from the ranch on the south Big Sur coast where she lived with her second husband, a retired physician. She looked to Group 4 as her re-entry career move. Another graduate of the University of California, Berkeley, journalism had been her vocation; a major avocation was championing architectural and environmental causes. By the time Group 4 came into being, she'd been in league with conservationists throughout the state helping to preserve California's scenic Big Sur coastline. She served on the Citizens' Advisory Committee for the Big Sur Master Plan and was a founding member of the Big Sur Land Trust, the Big Sur Foundation, and the Foundation for Environmental Design. A favorite quotation from M.F.K. Fisher—"The purpose of life is to grow old enough to have something to say"—underscored her eagerness to face a new challenge and possibly return to the kind of work she had put on hold after she remarried, became the stepmother of five, and settled on a mountain top.

**ILENE TUTTLE**, seventy-two, artist, arts consultant, and community-events planner, was already happily pursuing a multi-faceted re-entry career of her own design. A graduate of the University of California at Berkeley, with a BA in

Latin American Studies, Ilene is married to a retired attorney, a law student she met while in college. The mother of three grown sons, she had been designing and directing art programs, organizing civic events, and raising funds for non-profits for nearly twenty years. She had just completed an assignment for the Monterey Bay Aquarium, and knew the nearby office was available. Her aim was to use it as a base for her own work: with a recently retired husband, space at home was limited. When the idea of forming an association with other women who were all old friends came along, she felt it was time to settle in, assess the group's resources and talents, and explore the possibilities for action.

---

When the typewriters and file cabinets were in place, pencils sharpened, posters on the wall, and coffeepot perking, the question still hung in the air: "What did we *really* think we might develop as a joint effort?" We met in the office twice a week and talked about our mutual yearnings for greater self-satisfaction. We ultimately realized that this "something" we were talking about and searching for was probably *the* subject we needed to focus on! Then we asked ourselves, what had brought us to this point? Why were we still wanting *more?* Were there women who shared our view that growing older might hold opportunities for innovation? Ethel Barrymore said: "A good life is like a good play—it has to have a satisfying and exciting third act." We decided to investigate ways to write our own scenarios.

We started by examining the fact that we are members of a changed society. Statistically, by the year 2000 and for the first time in history, older people will outnumber the young. A majority will be women past mid-life, with a significantly longer life expectancy than any previous generation. What are they planning to do with these bonus years;

how will they remain productive, able to cope while realizing their dreams? We sought mentors and role models, data and guidebooks. What we discovered was a surprising lack of information about older women, but excellent exemplars in many disciplines and professions: women who were recognized barrier-breakers in a variety of fields, active, highly motivated, and singularly independent. They would live thirty years longer than their grandmothers and were spending this "gift of time" in challenging and fulfilling ways. Might their experience and attitudes provide clues for all of us in seeking new directions in our later years?

We wondered if we could assemble a group of these women, discuss a variety of topics, and produce a body of information that could be of value to women of *all* ages. We knew, for example, that historically women of our generation had repressed or set aside personal dreams to become mothers, wives, and workers. Would they view the thirty years they had left to live as an opportunity to "take their turn," to realize deferred ambitions? *Many* women fear being old, ill, or poor. Could more assertive planning while younger reduce this very real anxiety? And what about the concern that a woman past middle age might slide into a state of stagnation—becoming bored, or worse, *boring*?

How do American women hurdle the obstacles, shape their own destinies, and pursue challenging careers and interests into their sixties, seventies, eighties, even their nineties? For our pre-menopausal daughters and sisters seeking information about the after-fifty changes they anticipate in their bodies, health, careers, and lifestyles, might the views of "those who've been there" yield welcome guidelines?

We determined to call on multi-talented women who had risen to the top of a variety of professional disciplines to talk about what they have in common, and how their views might define, for the first time, a *new* older woman, one who welcomes challenge over leisure pursuits. But first we had to decide how and where we might assemble a group of such high achievers.

Our combined experience told us that fifteen was a practical number for the kind of intimate, sustained conversations we envisioned, and an invitational meeting seemed the perfect format for achieving this. A possible site emerged when we learned that Esalen Institute, a conference facility and spa on the Big Sur coast just an hour-long drive south of Monterey, had initiated a new program of week-long invitational workshops at a private residence on the grounds known as the Big House.

Esalen is noted for its spectacular setting overlooking the Pacific with natural hot springs, mineral baths, and rambling structures set among pines on a high bluff above the creeks and coves. Over the years it has been equally recognized for its devotion to sponsoring innovative thinking by attracting serious academic inquiry in a host of mind-stretching areas from inner-body and spiritual subjects to economics and anthropology.

The women we hoped to draw from across the country would be familiar with all the nuances of the offerings that make up "The Esalen Way"—the informal, open-ended, free-ranging discourse, the healthy vegetarian menu, the hot baths and physical therapy for which it has become famous. And we candidly admitted that they might be drawn equally by the dramatic scenery of the Big Sur coast. To our fledgling group, it seemed an atmosphere tailored to our needs—the perfect setting for a gathering of women. To our delight, the proposal for a one-week invitational conference the following summer brought a quick and affirmative response. We learned that *The New Older Woman: A Dialogue for the Coming Century* would be the first all-woman meeting convened at Esalen in its thirty-year history. (Ultimately, we were to hold two conferences at Esalen; a second one in 1992 would repeat the format, with a new guest list.)

Our invitation to the forum outlined our objectives: "To develop a seedbed and suggestions for future sustained dialogue; to identify commonalties facing women over age fifty; to produce a possible pilot for participation by a broader audience; to propose ways women can learn to plan ahead for changing life patterns; and to do this by inviting eleven American women of accomplishment from many disciplines to offer their viewpoints." We offered no stipends, honoraria, or travel expenses, causing more sophisticated conference planners to advise us that we'd never attract the women on our wish-list (including a three-time Emmy Award winner, two best-selling authors, the record-holder for the deepest ocean dive, and a Washington insider through two administrations) without these traditional enticements. But all of these women attended.

We wish to stress that we selected invitees for the forums with a singular purpose: to begin an inquiry process, to bring together articulate women who would be ready to speak up, experts in their fields who could identify and synthesize issues and who had experience in breaking down traditional walls. A larger, more demographically representative scope, while obviously wanting attention, was beyond our capabilities at this point. We felt that we needed to establish boundaries in order to make a start with any hope of achieving cogent results. We needed to build the foundation before we could expand. We told the potential participants there would be no set agenda, no research needed or asked for, no preparation of any kind. They were to come with themselves, not a briefcase. Our first acceptances came from two writers coming at women's concerns from two perspectives—the social and the scientific: anthropologist Catherine Bateson and best-selling author, Gail Sheehy. It gave us heart that the skeptics were wrong. And then, responding from all corners of the country, other invitees promptly and enthusiastically answered that they were keen to explore the uncharted territory the dialogues envisioned. None who accepted made any mention of remuneration.

We pondered our bonanza: what had *really* enticed these powerhouses to come from all parts of the country at their own expense to talk about being *new older women*? Was it the subject matter, the place, the list of the other invitees we had provided? Or was it the fact that we offered a forum where they could speak to other women outside their professions, "let their hair down" with women their own age without advance research or papers and speeches to deliver?

Whatever the lure, it was confidence-building for the four of us. Thus emboldened, we put out feelers to see if the media might care to learn of our plans. Our initial efforts to attract a feature story in major newspapers and magazines elicited a cutting rejection from the feature's editor of a major west-coast paper. She shot back a note: "*No use for older women—even those who are* new!" Another sent a message, "We'll pass." A communication from Frances Lear, publisher of Lear's, a magazine "for the woman who wasn't born yesterday," put it this way: "*Why should I write about older women? Their problems are the same as younger women's.*" We didn't believe these particular points of views because we had begun to believe in ourselves. Our instincts told us that the subject we'd chosen for a forum needed airing—that a gathering of women of our age talking together informally and non-competitively would be productive.

And that's exactly what happened. Conversations stretched

over five days in the summers of 1991 and 1992, with two three-hour sessions each day interspersed with hikes in neighboring woods, hot tubs, massage, and late-night gatherings of varying numbers before the fire or at the kitchen table. In all, twenty-six women (Group 4 plus eleven invitees each year) formed the assembly of accomplished women speaking out about everything that touched their lives—candidly, with humor, wisdom, and occasionally, anger. We limited the scope of our inquiry with the guest list; in so doing, we acknowledge the absence of views from women of diverse social, economic, ethnic or cultural backgrounds. But we believe that while the opinions we present are from a select group, the insights they reveal are of interest and relevance—recognizable to women everywhere. We have orchestrated their voices to define and inspire "The *New* Older Woman." We hope they will become familiar friends as the conversations progress.

## THE PARTICIPANTS

**Ruth Asawa**, 69
*Artist, Teacher* • San Francisco, CA
She welds, casts, and muscles metals as if they were dough—which, in fact, is another favorite medium for this accomplished sculptor, painter, and teacher. An artistic sensibility was a perspective we wanted—and needed. Thanks to Ruth, we saw how a creative mind views the world, translating the ordinary into extraordinary observations in color, texture, and form.

**Mary Catherine Bateson**, Ph.D., 55
*Anthropologist, Author, Professor* • Fairfax, VA
  The daughter of anthropologists Margaret Mead and Gregory Bateson, Catherine's arrival at Esalen had the aspect of
  a homecoming, having visited her father while he was
  scholar-in-residence at the Institute during the last years of
  his life. Assured and articulate, her perspective on the role
  of women in a historical as well as a contemporary context
  was invaluable.

**Virginia Boyak**, Ph.D., 68
*Industrial Gerontologist* • Santa Rosa, CA
  Whatever an "industrial gerontologist" is supposed to look
  like, we weren't prepared for Dr. "Ginny" Boyak. Tall,
  tanned, strikingly handsome, her quintessentially California
  looks marked her as an avid outdoorswoman. Embracing
  everything around her with radiant optimism, she generated
  megavolts of contagious, positive energy.

**Ruth Brinker**, 73
*Community Activist* • San Francisco, CA
  When we first met Ruth for lunch in San Francisco, we
  were prepared for a candle in the darkness; what we found
  was a laser in the light. Her sweet face and gentle de-
  meanor masked the toughness and organizational genius
  that brought her and Project Open Hand landmark status.
  Her spirit and profound faith were essential, we felt, to
  our dialogues.

**Denise Scott Brown**, 63
*Architect, Urban Planner* • Philadelphia, PA
  We agreed that an architect would be a particular asset to our
  colloquy, believing that a woman's sensitivity and instincts

were of special value in shaping living structures and environments. Denise was reported to be tough, outspoken, and exceptionally talented in this male-dominated profession. She took time out from a killer schedule for a detour to California, and we were all the richer for her contributions.

## Libby Cater, 69
*Former White House Assistant* • Montgomery, AL

Two powerful, high-profile women in the field of political communications insisted Libby would add savvy and sensitivity to our Esalen mix. They were right. She became our Washington insider with an outsider's penchant for fresh perspectives. With her soft Southern drawl and infectious laugh, it was easy to imagine her gracing a diplomatic dinner—and almost impossible to envision her in the center of Machiavellian in-fighting.

## Sylvia Earle, Ph.D., 59
*Marine Scientist* • Oakland, CA

Any of the seven seas are as much home to Sylvia as the golden rolling hills of Northern California where she presides over two corporations designing vehicles and technology for marine exploration. She was attending a meeting of the National Oceanic and Atmospheric Administration in Washington D.C. as our conference began and joined us a few days late, characteristically eager to shift gears to another kind of exploration.

## Claire Falkenstein, 87
*Artist* • Venice, CA

Claire was a legend as far back as our college days—especially in the Bay Area, where she established a reputation in the 1950s as a major talent in contemporary sculpture, painting, and design. She was initially apprehensive about our invitation, considering herself neither "new" nor "older." Nonetheless, a natural curiosity led to her acceptance, and she arrived well-stocked with sketch pads and strong opinions.

## Cecelia Hurwich, Ph.D., 75
*Research Psychologist* • Berkeley, CA

A *San Francisco Examiner* feature story alerted us to Cecelia's doctoral study of ten older women, *Vital Women in Their 70s, 80s, and 90s*, which promised a wealth of data on our subject. A walking reference desk on the New Older Woman, she met all our expectations as an advocate, expert, and role model.

## Sally Lilienthal, 75
*Human Rights and Peace Activist* • San Francisco, CA

Sally put a different spin on the idea of empowerment and, in the process, revealed something of herself and the status of widowhood. Her attitudes and opinions had an intensity of feeling and commitment that were reflected in her long dedication to the anti-war movement, political and sociological issues, and the arts.

## Mildred Mathias, Ph.D., 89
*Professor of Botany* • Los Angeles, CA

Mildred brought us back down to earth—quite literally—day after day. After our picnic lunches, she eagerly set off up the canyon paths, anxious to introduce us to "the natives" —the plants and flowers, that is. As she explained how each fern and fungus played its own unique role in the grand yet fragile ecosystems of Big Sur, our chosen roles in our own lives came into sharp and poignant focus.

## Elizabeth Mullen, 66
*Director, Women's Initiative AARP* • Washington D.C.

Peggy met "Bette" when she interviewed her for a book on women's interest groups. Her reaction to Bette was—"She's dynamite!" Bette has prioritized, analyzed, and interpreted various issues for AARP to over 19 million women, all over fifty-five. In the presence of her direct gaze, no one doubts she could mobilize this army if called upon.

## Judith Paige, R.D., 57
*Nutritionist, Author, Fashion Model* • Weston, MA

Even in baggy sweats, Judith looks like the fashion model she is—one of the top women over fifty in her profession. We were all anxious to meet this accomplished author, licensed dietician, yoga instructor, and lecturer on nutrition. She shared her personal experiences and refreshing views with a matter-of-fact optimism uniquely her own.

## Jane Porcino, Ph.D., 71
*Gerontologist, Author* • New York, NY

To say that Jane arrived at Esalen ready to rock and roll would be an understatement. Her enthusiasm and expertise (including two best-selling books) gave a positive charge to the group from the moment our dialogues began. Her ready smile warmed the foggy mornings while her impressive store of knowledge on the lives of older people in our society brought an informed and practical perspective.

## Judy Reemtsma, 59
*Television Producer* • New York, NY

When the credits roll for some of the most powerful TV documentaries of our time, chances are you'll see the credit: Judith Towers Reemtsma—Producer. One of her three

Emmys is broken, but she is moving much too fast to have it repaired. At Esalen, Judy was self-contained, focused, and down to earth — her opinions were uncensored and went directly to the heart of the matter at hand.

### Gail Sheehy, 57
*Author* • New York, NY

All four of us had redefined and remapped our lives after reading Gail Sheehy's *Passages* in the 1970s. Her book was a watershed for millions, and since then Gail has become a media star. Yet when asked to describe herself on our first night at Esalen, she said simply: "Sheehy...it's a good name for our times...two genders back to back." This was our introduction to her disarmingly feisty, tomboy sense of humor. The aggressive, hard-edged pro that we half-expected was, in fact, a deliciously funny, unselfconscious peer.

### Mary Louise Smith, 81
*National Republican Party Leader* • Des Moines, IA

She made history in 1974 as the first woman to chair the National Republican Party, but had already earned the label "veteran political pro" as a life-long campaign worker who had come through the volunteer ranks in her home state. Mary Louise was the dream image of the wise confidant. Gracefully eschewing the floor cushions for a chair by the corner windows, her perfectly coiffed silver hair aglow against the incoming light—everyone fell in love with Mary Louise.

### Irene Tinker, Ph.D., 68
*Professor of City Planning, Women's Studies* • Berkeley, CA

As one of the few conference attendees who had taken the academic track in an unbroken move to her doctorate, she has combined scholarship with activism throughout her career. With short white hair and a quiet reticence, Irene listened intently and contributed forcefully in the area of women in other cultures, insisting on a global focus to our discussions.

### Harriett Woods, 68
*President, National Women's Political Caucus* • St. Louis, MO
Harriett was scheduled to be the next president of the National Women's Political Caucus when we extended our invitation. By the time she arrived at Esalen, the day after her election, the media was in hot pursuit. She politely evaded them. Our conference offered her an interlude to unwind and reflect on the changes the coming year would bring, as well as chance to share her unique perspective with other women.

### Marilyn Yalom, 63
*Professor of French, English Literature* • Palo Alto, CA
As Senior Research Scholar at Stanford's prestigious Institute for Research on Women and Gender, we were honored when Marilyn agreed to join our discussions, and grateful to her for supplying a historical framework. She educated us on the real circumstances of Western women a hundred and more years ago, helping us see how far we had come, yet reminding us how far we have still to go.

### Gwen Yeo, Ph.D., 61
*Gerontologist* • Palo Alto, CA
We particularly wanted Gwen to be a part of the conference for her solid academic background in gerontology. A non-stuffy academic whose light touch brought relief to some heavy moments, she validated premises, contradicted or corrected with a genial air, and kept us honest and reasonably on track.

**Eleanor Zuckerman**, Ph.D., 62
*Clinical Psychologist* • San Francisco, CA

An advocate who gets results when she adopts a cause, Ellie's practical style and engagingly articulated opinions make her a role model with accomplishments only dreamed of by less focused idealists. While at Esalen, her expert views and observations were laced with wit, logic, and her own unique clarity of vision.

# CHAPTER ONE

# Enter the New Older Woman

Ready or not, here she is, undefined in either academic or popular terms until now: the New Older Woman.

She is unique in many ways. For one, she will live thirty years longer than her grandmother. Her daughters will live even longer. She was born on the cusp of the Roaring Twenties and in the years leading to the Great Depression. Her life will stretch well beyond the year 2000. No one pointed out to her that she would have this gift of time, nor was society prepared for her. But even if she wasn't announced, she certainly was not prepared to have to struggle so hard for visibility in a culture geared to ever-youthfulness.

The world doesn't fit her anymore—nor do its clothes, medical knowledge, attitudes, living spaces. Indeed, society seems a little embarrassed to find her still here. Historically speaking, she should be dead.

She is not only alive, but kicking.

## THE CONVERSATIONS BEGIN

*"I've never been invited to talk about my own feelings as a woman..."*

Arriving by auto and airport limo after a forty-five-mile drive down the winding coastal road, the invitees' travel-fatigued

nerves are considerably soothed with a view of their home-
to-be for the coming week. Reached by a foot bridge, the
Big House at Esalen Institute lies across a rocky ravine from
the center's main grounds. The two-story sprawling wood
structure dominates a broad grassy expanse of gardens, aged
cypress trees, and steep paths leading down the cliff to
the sea below. Our meetings take place in the large living
room with windows overlooking the Pacific; huge pillows
heaped on the floor are the only furniture and are ideal for
a casual discussion.

On the first day, as participants file into the living room,
there's a palpable uncertainty in the early morning air.
Mary Catherine Bateson, who prefers to be called Catherine, zeroes in on it right away. Settling into a pile of pillows,
she wants definition: "Every conference I've ever been to—
and I've been to hundreds—I've had to lead a workshop or
give a speech. I've never been invited to come and just talk
about my own feelings as a woman. How do we do this? It
sounds very intriguing."

Those who are accustomed to academic life nod. We get
our first hint that the need for structure or objectives might
get periodic airings in the coming days.

On the other hand, Denise Scott Brown, tossing her gray
bobbed hair, has no doubts. "I know precisely why I'm here.
How could I not be? As an older woman architect operating
in what is still, in its upper echelons, a man's field, I seldom
have a chance to talk with a group of women my age about
being a woman. I was curious, and I couldn't pass up the
opportunity. And it took some doing; having just arrived
home in Philadelphia from business in London the day
before yesterday, I feel as though I've been in the air for
a week!"

Other women join in, voicing their interest in the discussions to come, and gradually a sense of commonality and

receptivity takes over. These women begin to feel free to say what is in their hearts—to unburden their minds with no reticence.

## THE HISTORICAL PERSPECTIVE

*"Forty was the beginning of old age for women in the Nineteenth Century..."*

PATRICIA FAUL (PAT), sets the stage for the examination of the "New Older Woman" by looking at the past, specifically with a description of a Western woman one hundred years ago:

"She was either married or the designated caretaker of her aging parents. Her actuarial age of death was forty-eight, compared to our seventy-eight. She had given birth to an average of eight children. History books and novels written in the late 1800s did little or nothing to describe the daily routine of the average housewife. Keeping the household running was extremely labor-intensive for those who could not afford hired help. Just delivering food to the table was an enormous task without the conveniences of refrigeration and preservation we have today. I imagine how my mother, operating a ranch and rearing five children while Dad worked in an office, would have coveted a microwave, a freezer, a dishwasher. Or how today's medical advances might have benefited her stressful routine. She died at fifty-seven of a massive heart attack. Hormone replacement therapy might have saved her.

"Clothing one hundred years ago, and in the Great Depression, was hand- or machine-sewn; laundry and ironing were grueling and laborious. It takes no stretch of the imagination to understand why—dead-tired, with never-ending tasks, and no independent life to claim—women died at forty-eight. If she was lucky enough to survive childbirths and infections, she might have a chance for longer life, but it was one of continued servitude. The many men who became widowers sought competent mates; after all, they needed someone to run the household."

MARILYN YALOM is champing at the bit. As a specialist in Victorian women and women in French literature, this is her territory, and she jumps right in: "Forty was considered the beginning of old age in the nineteenth century, so everything after that was the decline of life. When you were forty you were old. Women's lives were conceptualized as two critical periods — *critical* was the term used in the literature. They were puberty and menopause. Girls entered into puberty at their risk and peril, and they got through menopause — *if* they got through — also at their risk and peril.

"So today, when I hear the phrase 'middle age,' I think, 'the middle of *what*'? If we're thinking of a one-hundred-year pattern, maybe middle age would really have some meaning if we thought of it as being between about forty to sixty. But that period keeps shifting. Those years from sixty to eighty, those are the hardest to define. You've chosen the working definition 'the new older woman' for this forum. Well, I don't expect to resolve the issue, but it's obvious that we don't have a very clear-cut line of demarcation, not like people did in the last century. Then menopause marked the beginning of the end for women. In many societies you began to wear black and you wore it for the rest of your life. You were not expected to remarry if you became a widow."

ILENE TUTTLE: "Unless, of course, you married a widower, put your children with his, and doubled the housewife's burden."

MARILYN: "Oh yes, and it made sense in some ways to define women as reproductive beings because so much of their lives were given over to producing and caring for babies. The Victorian woman's life as described in fiction and non-fiction was written by men. But there is nothing written by women, certainly nothing in the medical literature. There were virtually no women doctors. Some of the medical literature is grim if you read it now; you realize how very biased it was. Some of the French doctors sounded like Renaissance poets lamenting the loss of women's charm — and, what's worse, drew the relationship between menopause and mental illness, and how one could become querulous, peevish, and deranged."

MARY CATHERINE BATESON (CATHERINE): "What it seems to me we're discussing here, and Marilyn raised this in her opening, is 'What is it that we really believe about the life cycle?' Do we believe that old age has changed?"

JUDY REEMTSMA rings a bell we've heard before when she observes, "I've never really thought about myself as a 'New Older Woman'…I've just always gone through life with my own series of frustrations, not really knowing what I'm supposed to do next." It's hard to believe. At the peak of her professional powers as a television producer, how can this calm, down-to-earth, feet-on-the-ground sophisticate confess to any frustrations—let alone a series of them? Alert and compact, with dark bangs framing a thoughtful face, she seems to us to epitomize East Coast confidence and *savoir faire*. She listens intently, and when she speaks, her quiet style, directness, and sharp sense of humor cut to the heart of the subject.

Others identify with Judy's outlook. Most of us have been too busy doing whatever we do to worry about getting old —or *being* old. Successively (sometimes simultaneously), we've been preoccupied with learning, working, loving, getting married, making homes and babies, building or reentering careers, expanding relationships, coping with changes, and meeting new crises—celebrating and sorrowing. Old age: what is that? Maybe those women's magazine and newspaper editors were right. It hasn't been part of *our* agenda either. Until now.

CATHERINE: "I think it's important to determine whether the blankness people have about certain ages is a characteristic of the life cycle: you can't know what something's going to be like until you get there. Whether it has something to do with the way we construct the future in general or the idea of old age is unclear. I think that as children we often had quite clear ideas of what life was going to be like when we 'grew up'—which was usually sixteen or eighteen—of what it would be like to be married. I think it's an interesting phenomenon that older people feel very short of models, very short of imaging constructions of what it's going to be like to be sixty, eighty, ninety. These images aren't there. They're just not available."

The subject of Catherine's book, *Composing a Life* (Dutton, 1989), is how women deal with the multiple priorities that shape their existence. She says, "Today, the materials and skills from which a life is composed are no longer clear. It is no longer possible to follow the paths of previous generations. It is especially true for women, whose whole lives no longer need be dominated by the rhythms of procreation and the dependencies that these created, but who must still live with the discontinuities of female biology and still must balance conflicting demands. Our lives not only take new directions, they are subject to repeated redirection, partly because of the extension of our years of health and productivity."

GAIL SHEEHY: "You know, people in their late thirties and forties have this terrific hurry-up feeling, like everything's got to be done right away because they're coming to the end of the old age of youth—whereas I think of the fifties as the youth of old age. It's as if you get another burst—another extension of life. You've made it to that point, and you feel healthy and vital."

We continue to talk about the extent to which we've accepted the reality of being "senior citizens" (a term most of us find distasteful), but it's been with some amusement along with disbelief and perhaps, dismay. We enjoy the perks: lower fares and ticket prices, larger type, easier access and preferential seating—sometimes even old-fashioned courtesy and respect. But we also feel the occasional pique at the manner in which they're proffered. After all those years of being made to produce I.D.s when we were kids— to prove you were eighteen, then twenty-one—*now* we're being carded to prove we're sixty, sixty-five or older!

In researching this subject, we found that our generation has identified the female passages as the onset of "the curse" and "the change," with childbearing somewhere in the middle. Menstruation marks the dawning of sexuality, menopause its sunset. Historically, the passage into young womanhood has been joyously celebrated in music, art, and poetry—more contemporaneously by confirmations, bat mitzvahs, quinzes, coming-out parties, cotillions, and other ceremonial rites introducing the virgin to the tribe. Menopause—euphemistically, the change of life—has been a taboo topic largely memorialized in jokes about hot flashes. The ignorance, superstition, and apprehension that has surrounded menopause is beginning to be demystified, its physiological and psychological complexities explained. Estrogen therapy has mitigated many of its discomforts and depressions, and more knowledgeable practitioners and effective medications are now available to ease the passage.

PAT: "If we now have thirty additional years of relatively good health, could we define the New Older Woman's time span as post-menopausal to pre-frailty—or to death, since many never really become frail in their minds?"

MARILYN: "When we conceptualize or construct models for humans, we almost always start with some kind of male model. Even now, when we talk about the years from sixty to eighty or thereafter, we think of that as retirement. Retiring from what? From a *male* life cycle—which, for most women has not been their experience. Although we, here, represent women who have had more paid employment than most women, if we are to come up with some kind of model, I really would want it to correspond more closely to what the experiences of women actually are."

In further discussion, participants felt that to some, this passage implies rest and retirement: a time to relax and savor the pleasures of grandchildren or gardening, enjoy new options with more time for friends, and unhurried travels. Others choose to remain in jobs or careers as long as they are able. A shared view is that it offers opportunity to accept new challenges: running for public office, mentoring other women, engaging in community service, going back to school—taking up where one left off when motherhood and marriage intervened. The New Older Woman is characterized as one who deliberately or intuitively brings together the bits and pieces of her life to create a quilt, a mosaic, what Catherine calls "composing a life."

CATHERINE: "There really are two fundamental installments to being an adult. There are the reproductive years, and then some kind of transition that goes with menopause which is *not* the transition to old age: rather it's a transition to a second adulthood. *Then* there will be a transition to old age."

That second adulthood is what women didn't have one hundred years ago.

## WHAT'S *NEW* ABOUT HER?

*"No more wondering, 'Is this right?'...The older I get, the more confidence I enjoy."*

VIRGINIA MUDD: "Now that we've established a chronological age niche for her, what else can we say about the 'new older woman' that makes her so different from any women before her?"

Gail is poised with yellow legal pad and pencil. She admits she's gathering notes for her forthcoming book on menopause.

GAIL: "I stopped *Passages* (William Morrow & Co., 1981), a book about the stages of life, at age fifty because I couldn't envision anything past fifty. I came to this conference thinking, 'Well, they told me I'm going to be the 'baby' of the group. I'm really enthusiastic about joining it as the youngest member; I'll feel comfortable in representing the *younger* viewpoint.' It turns out that I'm *not* the youngest. Catherine inches me out by a year, but that's sort of nice. Actually, what's happening here is that I'm feeling completely overshadowed by the over-seventies and over-eighties and how beautiful and rich and vital you are. I'm thinking there's a whole new determination that I must have in order to develop in a way that the later period of my life *will* involve choice. So, I do feel like the 'baby' in terms of crawling and learning from all of you.

"Now I realize I wasn't ready to be fifty until I was fifty-two—I'd been so busy running. I picture myself as this little kid racing against boys five or six and having to win. Now I'm confronting this over-achiever who, I realize, has been running for her life all her life. I'm aware of looking for my future self, and I think that's something women in their fifties begin to do. I think it's a useful thing to do, through groups of women who are at the same age and older...what we're doing here."

CECELIA HURWICH is ready to offer insights gained from her interviews with ten "old" women she interviewed for her longitudinal study published in 1990, the result of a ten-year doctoral research project. "My premise was to study women over seventy who seemed to be enjoying their later lives, who were admired by their friends and community in Berkeley, California, and who had a zest for living. I put out a call and received hundreds of names. Hundreds! If a name came in more than one time, I got a little biographical sketch of each person and sent a letter: 'Would you be interested in talking to me?' This was the experience of my life because I found that these remarkable women had all sorts of reasons for *not* being active: some of them had arthritis, or they'd been in and out of cancer, but they were living fully and enjoying themselves. And contributing something."

PAT: "What did the age group have in common?"

CECELIA: "They were all vitally involved in something that was of compelling interest to them — peace activities, the environment, the writing of an autobiography, continuation of their career, or mentoring younger people...each had a consuming interest she pursued right into her seventies and eighties, even though many of them weren't driving or highly mobile. I interviewed them again, ten years later, when the oldest one was ninety-five and the youngest eighty-one. Regretfully, some of them have since died. I had become attached."

ILENE: "What single factor do you think sets these women apart?"

CECELIA: "It seems they all came to a point sometime in their fifties when they stopped trying to hang on to youth and anticipated the opportunity to move on. I learned that, number one, being involved in something you believe in is primary, something that gives you a sense of self, something outside yourself. Not me and mine. Not my kids and my grandkids and my house. Not that kind of stuff. None of the women I worked with was wealthy; I don't think they were ever materialistic or consumer oriented. They were not big TV watchers; they were big readers. They chose correspondence and the telephone to keep in touch."

VIRGINIA: "Did any use a computer?"

CECELIA: "No. Not one. But I asked them about that, and got a very smart answer from one: 'I like to concentrate on things that are confidence building. I'm *going* to get at the computer and I'm going to get some young person to show me and I'm going to feel very dumb, I know. It's a risk.' They were nonconformists. Highly individual. They all married because it was expected of them. A third had divorced, another third was still married, and one third was widowed. A theme in their lives was a closeness with nature; one woman called it the 'wilderness of the psyche.' They were all avid gardeners. As a group, they felt far less concerned about death and growing older than they had in their fifties."

DENISE: "What about missing a dead spouse? If they're so busy living in the present, does it mean they don't feel the lack of a person they've lived with all their lives?"

CECELIA: "No. They miss them, but somehow they've gone on and continued a very fulfilling life. That's another thing: they have many friends of all ages. That's important—to have younger as well as older acquaintances. You ask for commonalities: I found good health habits, remaining in one's own home, having a variety of friends—young and old—and staying connected to the daily goings-on of the world."

CATHERINE: "So far we've defined the New Older Woman by her extended lifespan, and by the necessary elasticity, or improvisation, she has been forced to bring to her life. Cecelia has given us an insight into ways older women successfully maintain their vitality. But we also need to think of chronological age in contrast to professional age, or caretaking age. Where a woman is in relation to these age layers has to do with her self-selected reproductive years. Today, women can be professionally young if they enter or re-enter the marketplace later in life. They can elect maternity at an age when our mothers were coming down the home-stretch. Great-grandchildren are a part of their lives—not their afterlives. The life cycles that controlled our mothers' time are being manipulated, warped, and re-shaped."

GAIL: "The shape of the life cycle has changed dramatically in the years since I finished *Passages*. People are taking longer to grow up and longer to die and that changes all the shapes and options in between. I'd like to know how women feel about their sense of self in relation to others: spouse, children, parents, deceased parents, younger women associates or competitors. I'd like to know about the relative safety and danger in their lives, and which areas seem safer or more secure. We may feel starting something new at age seventy is absolutely smashing, and 'why not?' But there is always this pull that says, 'This is not quite right—this is a little bizarre—this is out of the ordinary.'"

CATHERINE: "We wouldn't say it was smashing if we didn't have a set of expectations that we'd inherited from an earlier era. The tone of voice in which people talk about it expresses the fact that they're under the influence of an earlier set of ideas about the life cycle. I think those earlier ideas are quite oppressive; people make decisions on the basis of them. They use them as a lens."

RUTH BRINKER voices agreement. A compassionate and impassioned community activist, quiet and profoundly spiritual, she knows firsthand the barriers conventional views place in one's path. She has a soft-spoken manner that punctuates the dialogue, inviting serious attention.

RUTH B.: "I think that people have been stuck in stereotypes. You reached sixty-five and you were automatically retired and it was time to get your membership in the senior citizen's center; and then you were encouraged to play golf or whatever. None of it was ever necessary. People have always had the energy to do more serious things and they just didn't have the courage to break out of the mold they felt society was forcing them into. Women coming along behind us will be less weighted by the baggage of doing it the way it's always been done. Certainly, yes, that era is *over!*"

CATHERINE: "We're underestimating the extent of the change we're in the middle of. When I turned fifty, I thought it was the best birthday I'd ever had because it suddenly dawned on me that, having expected my life to be essentially over at fifty like the statistics describe, there was, in fact, probably as much to come as there had been before! At that point, I could empathize with people for whom a fiftieth birthday was absolutely the knell of doom and at the same time see things another, happier way."

Confirming Catherine's optimism, Claire Falkenstein, at eighty-four, is ardent in her belief that her later years are affording her greater freedom, self assurance, and recognition in terms of her creative output than ever before. She excitedly describes her recently conceived view of her life's work: an art vocabulary she calls the "never-ending screen," dealing with eternity and infinity, which translates not only in her work, but as a definition of her age and place in that flow.

CLAIRE FALKENSTEIN: "I've never, up to now, been able to use a symbolic language in the way I do now; now isn't that great? I've never been able to do that before, and what's interesting to me about it is that I have absolutely no lack of confidence. I'm *absolutely* confident in what I'm doing; I feel 'This is right to do.' As a young person, you're always wondering, 'Is this right?' or 'Am I evolving?' But that's all over. It's happened over the last five years, since I turned eighty! The older I get, the more confidence I enjoy."

Claire's enthusiasm is echoed by botanist Mildred Mathias. Exuding hearty good cheer, she is every inch the academic explorer who enjoys the companionship of a wide circle of younger friends, who, she claims, continue to "charge her batteries."

MILDRED MATHIAS: "I used to say when I was doing fieldwork in the Amazon that every summer I spent there probably added ten years to my life. My mother died at ninety-seven and was active until about ninety-four, so I think I have a fair chance of reaching one hundred. Actually, it's confirmed statistically that people who are engaged in scientific field work have greater longevity than people in other occupations."

CATHERINE: "I think there's a whole dimension here that ties up with our earlier discussions of why older women remain energetic and productive...and it is this: in order to care for a family, you have to maintain a system of some sort; you're not just responding with compassion. You're building, organizing, and getting involved. Women are moving from a kind of personal caring in the microcosm to caring more broadly, and Mildred is showing that it can be expressed through the building of institutions whose mission is caring globally...about the biosphere."

MILDRED: "I've constantly shifted emphasis on things...in a way, it has been opportunistic: 'Oh, well, here's another challenge.' When I was seventy-two, I took on an assignment to organize a national office for a botanical association. It was supposed to take about two years; it took four. I had to learn new things—how to complete IRS reports, write grants."

HARRIETT WOODS, an energetic woman with a lifelong commitment to public service, also recognizes the importance of learning new things as Mildred speaks of them.

HARRIETT: "When you talk about caregiving and building

institutions, I find it's a continual learning process for any of us as older women...or at any age. Very often you have to get information to acquire new skills. I've noticed that in this group, we're still asking, 'How do you do this?' There are people who don't do things because they don't know how, and don't know how to learn."

Inevitably, as we continue talking, we see that the choices that define the New Older Woman and that are bringing satisfaction to our participants are shaped by circumstances: health and mobility, financial security (or lack of), and family situations. All members of this group share access to better medical and mental health care than ever before, as well as the newer phenomenon of support groups.

Some women discuss the powerful symbolism expressed in traditional rites of passage and the veneration of elders in ancient cultures and religions. Virginia noted the recent revival of the ceremony of "croning"—a celebration of a woman's passage into later life, and her initiation into becoming an elder. Marilyn describes a ritual she attended where the initiate was surrounded by family members and friends, both men and women. "There were flowers, candles, music...quite a wonderful phenomenon," she observes.

Some more pragmatic members find ideas such as "croning" a bit far-out. "Where I come from in the Midwest, this would just not be relevant," one observes. But others agree with Marilyn's speculation: "Maybe there's a place for the joyous idea that older people who have greater links to the past have something very important to offer."

CATHERINE: "If we take the terms—the 'virgin', the 'mother' and the 'crone'—the fact is that the term 'crone' did include some wise, hale, hearty old women who were in that category chronologically, but the image was determined by the state that most women that age were *really* in, their actual condition."

The liberating nature of the transition into a second adulthood offers women tempting opportunities for expanding individuality. Cecelia confirms that the vital older women she interviewed "prized non-conformity...they valued and cultivated eccentricity." Free of worrying "what others will think," a new rite of passage *permits* buying a sportscar at eighty, learning to fly at sixty, climbing Mt. Whitney at seventy or falling in love at eighty!

VIRGINIA: "So what *you* New Older Women are saying is that change—passages, transitions, cycles—are a result of, or influenced by, both longer life spans and shifting social attitudes about what *is* and what *is not* appropriate at any stage of life."

PAT: "And the changes you cite are having a profound impact. They set the stage for the New Older Woman—for the style in which she'll conduct herself, for the barriers she'll leap, and for the taboos she'll shed as she pursues her agenda and gets on with embracing the future."

## THE BRIDGE GENERATION: SPANNING THE GAP

*"I feel a strong sense of responsibility...a real obligation to help younger women overcome barriers."*

The conversation flows naturally to a discussion of today's older woman and of her relationships to the generations above and below her.

Peggy Downes pictures the New Older Woman standing, arms outstretched in opposite directions: "One hand is still linked to her mother, who transmits coded messages as to how she should define herself. The other hand reaches out to her daughter, passing on a dramatically altered set of possibilities and priorities. It feels at the same time awkward and exhilarating—this attempt to bridge an unprecedented 'expectations gap.' Imagined as a 'high-wire act,' it offers unique risk and reward, challenge and opportunity."

ILENE: "In a way, when her mother reached womanhood, the choices open to her were few and well-defined; maybe that was easier—options can be confusing."

PEGGY: "By the time the New Older Woman reaches midlife, many in her generation will have already forced open the doors marked 'Men Only.' In turn, her daughter will pass through these doors more gracefully, as a matter of right. For older women, it takes a special kind of guts—this opening of long-locked doors. The effort is often painful; it may exact a high price."

**BETTE MULLEN** responds to Peggy's observation: "The support and guidance of a caring mentor lowers that price, but for our generation, welcome and comfort in the workplace offered by one woman to another has been in short supply. Networks of women were, until recently, unimaginable. In many fields, role models simply did not exist; we were often forced to go it on our own."

JUDY states her case simply: "In the world of TV, when I began, I was it. There was no one to take me by the hand. I had to start from scratch."

**MARY LOUISE SMITH**, the first woman in history to head the Republican Party, speaks from experience: "There were no women mentors when I began my career in politics. There were only individual men who taught me the ropes... bottom-line organizational politics. Now, as a result, I feel a strong sense of responsibility—a real obligation to bring other women along, to help them overcome barriers."

Others mentioned that being a part of a "bridge generation" invites confrontation and an element of intergenerational conflict. The "connectors" are easy targets, "sitting ducks" for negative perceptions by both mothers and daughters. What is seen as strong and daring by the New

Older Woman may be interpreted by her mother as un-ladylike defiance and by her daughter as embarrassing eccentricity. More stressful still, the role of connector fosters tension within one's own generation. An example is the flap created when women re-entered the work force or become re-entry students rather than remain homemakers.

At a focus group facilitated by Group 4 at Vassar College in the spring of 1992, Peggy reports that members of the class of 1952 were asked how they perceived themselves in the midst of change. The class was unevenly split. About one quarter of the group viewed its generation as simply part of an incremental, smooth, and historical flow. The majority of women surveyed disagreed, describing themselves as being caught in a rough and unprecedented seachange.

We're in hearty agreement that there are some dilemmas associated with being part of a bridge generation: the New Older Woman has had few mentors, but is committed to mentoring the next generation; she has taken jobs where she's been dependent on an "old boys' network," but she's active in weaving support systems for other women. She may have undergone a no-fault divorce and witnessed the decline of the attitude that divorce presumes personal failure. She saw the invention of The Pill as a near-perfect birth control method. She remembered the Second World War, which allowed women into the national work force on a grand scale. Rosie the Riveter may have gone back home to be part of the baby boom, but she never forgot the exhilaration of meaningful work and her own paycheck.

The New Older Woman has grown up having to fight her way through some negative stereotypes. Her daughter will now find positive female role models in virtually every field. Her mother's health has been given cursory attention by the medical profession; her daughter will be the subject of longitudinal studies in every medical specialty, conducted by a host of both public and private agencies. Where her mother found many closed doors, her daughter is finding an array of opportunities. Anti-discrimination legislation, recent court decisions, and successful feminist challenges are assuring greater openness, equality, and opportunity for young women entering the work force.

The New Older Woman is curious and concerned about her connective role and committed to securing hard-won options and support systems for the next generation. Most importantly, she points to a new way of being for herself.

# CHAPTER TWO

# The Private Woman

As the days proceed, an increasing candor emerges among the participants. An atmosphere of trustfulness, and a willingness to share deeply-felt personal concerns, infuse the dialogue.

Deep within herself, each woman holds a life's accumulation of hopes and memories, fears and loves, joys and disappointments. Privately, she nurtures her self-confidence and resources to cope with the multiple demands on her energies. She's promised greater choices, better health, and longer life than women of preceding generations—but who will be there to share it? Increasingly, the answer is: other older women.

A common thread running through our dialogues is the concern for balancing the demands of one's public and professional life—including volunteer and societal obligations—with responsibilities of family. This may include husband, children, grandchildren, probably great-grandchildren, even frail parents who require caretaking. At this stage, a woman's relationship with her spouse also undergoes changes: he may be content with retirement, while she remains active; their sexual relationship may be equally out of balance. Outwardly functioning effectively in her multiple roles, a woman at this point often copes with fatigue, stress, and depression, resulting from concerns for her career as well as her personal life. Publicly, she projects confidence, competance, and strength; privately she may be unfulfilled or suffer a sense of inadequacy—even, at times, invisibility.

Along with her varying roles and obligations, the New Older Woman faces a new life change: menopause. The participants are keen to discuss and demystify this fact of female life, what Gail Sheehy calls "The Silent Passage," in her book of the same name (Random House, 1992).

### ALTERED STATES:
### INVISIBILITY AND EMPOWERMENT

*"When we put ourselves in situations where we have no comfortable way to connect, aren't we making ourselves more vulnerable to feeling invisible?"*

There's a loneliness and a loss of confidence that comes with feeling 'invisible'; on the other hand, going solo can be empowering. These antithetical aspects surface when the conversations turn to the older woman's deepest personal realities.

Gail calls it the Bag-Lady Complex, the atavistic fear evoked by the sight of a homeless old woman, her worldly possessions stuffed into shopping bags or a grocery cart, alone on the city streets: "We can't help but think, 'There, but for the grace of God, go I....'"

VIRGINIA BOYAK (GINNY): "In a post-doctoral study, I asked women: 'What is your greatest fear about getting old?' It was the same thing: 'Being alone, being sick, being poor,' which statistics show they have a good chance of being unless they're white, middle-class and educated: those are the three factors that skew that potential.

"There's something else besides financial concerns going on with a woman at that time of her life too: that is self-image. The issue invariably comes up with a divorce when the man is leaving the marriage for a younger woman. For most women that's devastating."

Many of the women acknowledge that loneliness and depression have sent some of them to counselors in times of stress. Divorcees and widows are especially vulnerable: "It's a couples' world out there,"one newly widowed member observes wistfully.

GWEN YEO: "New therapies, counseling, and interventions for older women have proved to be very helpful. On the whole, women over fifty are less prone to depression than any other age or gender group."

ELEANOR ZUCKERMAN (ELLIE): "With my women patients, much of their depression is for good reason—it comes at transitions in people's lives, when they are going to be asked to give up a lot. A lot of women have low-level depression and most of them have very specific causes. Sometimes, if a patient is happy, she feels guilty because of the disparity between herself and her mother. Often, it's a bad husband. Or, she may have reactivated grief from an earlier experience—usually related to feeling guilty for the unhappiness or suffering of the mother. So if you don't *know* whether you're depressed, don't worry about it!"

CLAIRE, who lives alone in her studio/home, has the strongest words on the subject: "The only way to go is to *go on*! I value my solitude, I welcome visitors, but I need to be alone and work through ideas. Passion's the word! You have to be passionate about what you're doing!"

GWEN: "When we put ourselves in new situations where we don't know people—getting out of our space, mingling in the world, and we have no comfortable way to connect—aren't we making ourselves even more vulnerable to feeling invisible?"

**IRENE TINKER:** "If you *really* want to be invisible, try walking down a street in a *chador* (the all-enveloping dark garment with eye-slits, worn by many Muslim women). Having done this for a day, I felt people maneuvering out of my way. After a while, you feel empowered *because* you're invisible: you could do anything—nobody knows who you are!"

GWEN: "We attribute to age things that don't have anything to do with age. We say we forget things 'because I'm getting old.' I think that's where our problems start, and we perpetuate them. Soon people expect it, the media reinforce it, then people become *gerontophobic*. This cycle gets repeated and gains momentum."

ELLIE: "We paste denigrating labels on images of women, and that's where *The Beauty Myth* (William Morrow & Co., 1991), message comes in. In her book, Naomi Wolf talks about the torture and confusion that's inflicted on even sophisticated women by societal views that physical beauty equates with security and success. You have to avoid the internalization of all these sorts of messages that society hands out."

**JUDITH PAIGE:** "The degree to which I assign the fact that I'm getting older to everyday things surprises me. It's a cop-out—a foolproof cop-out!" Judith's comments mirror her serious concern with women's issues in her parallel careers as dietician and New York fashion model.

JANE PORCINO: "The first time I was aware of this invisibility, I was at a geriatric meeting in Washington and I didn't know anyone there. I got all dressed up and went down to the reception alone and I couldn't get *anyone* to look at me—no eye contact at all; I wandered, I waited, I felt like the "Invisible Woman." I got so depressed, I was about to go back to my room, but I saw a man standing alone, so I went up to him and introduced myself. And he was a *lovely* man, and invited me to join his group…so it was all right."

IRENE: "This sort of thing happens all the time in Washington:

if you don't go up and talk to someone, you'll be out of it. As you get older, though, you have more confidence—it becomes easier."

Pat recalled a passage from Carolyn Heilbrun's book, *Writing a Woman's Life* (Ballentine, 1989), in which the author recounts an incident from a popular mystery story. The female character shoots a man, places the gun in her handbag, and leaves unnoticed because she's old. Later she's hired by the mob as a hit-woman because she's achieved the kind of invisibility the job requires. Heilbrun talks about the 'circle of invisibility' that women experience when they reach mid-life—when looks no longer count for so much. The worry that overcomes women at this stage is often painful.

ILENE: "It happens so fast, some women don't have time to agonize. Simone de Beauvoir said, 'They're all young, these people who suddenly find they are old.' She went on to say that one day she was forty, and by the time she recovered from the shock, she was fifty!"

JANE: "But the agony, as you call it, is real for the woman who is suffering. Maybe one of the most important things we can do for ourselves at times like that is to surround ourselves with people who care for us and for each other."

GWEN: "It's become uncomfortable to ask a woman what she does, if she answers that, by choice, she's 'just a housewife'. We don't have the social language for this yet, like: 'Do you work in the home, or do you get paid for your work?'"

LIBBY CATER turned the conversation from invisibility to empowerment and self-esteem. "As you get older, I think that when you center yourself—get comfortable with yourself, keep your mind open, keep your sense of wonder, try to learn and feel inner peace. You then have an aura and a presence that younger people notice, and they want to be with you. The things that turn you on will bring people to you. Norman Cousins talked a lot about the medical reasons for staying creative and productive: he said, 'Each time we choose half-involvement, we are also choosing partial death.'"

SALLY LILIENTHAL: "What empowered me—and I imagine it happened to a lot of others in this room—was not a job and not a career. It was a very personal reason and it had nothing to do with age. Yes, I had the security and freedom provided by financial means, and I was able to do whatever I wanted to do because I didn't have to worry about making a living. But I was brought up to think that men made the decisions, and when my loving husband died several years ago, I felt empowered. I don't think that's at all unusual for people of my age, do you?"

JANE: "I don't, not at all!...and it needs to be said. It's very different when men are there. It's not all downhill when they're not—for many women, it's empowerment for the first time!"

SALLY: "I had positions that were as big as I have today, professionally, but I didn't feel empowered until I was alone and didn't have a man to answer to."

ELLIE: "You need to have power! The people with the power are men. Men make the job appointments and do the hiring, and they would rather see cute young girls around the office... so they get their choice."

JANE: "Even if you look at a magazine like *Modern Maturity*, (monthly magazine published by the American Association of Retired Persons, Washington, D.C.), they may have stories about older people, but their ads always reinforce *The Beauty Myth* point of view...it maintains the power structure, the notion that we're only empowered when we're young and sexy."

ELLIE: "Men think women envy their penises. It's not that at all. Their power is what women envy!"

MARY LOUISE SMITH: "I'm in awe of all this! I always did what
    I wanted to do. I grew up in a rather disciplined family. We
    had breakfast, lunch, and dinner together. I never felt de-
    prived or restricted in any way, or unempowered. You did
    what you do in a small town: you headed the United Cru-
    sade, you ran for the school board and were elected; you
    did the things you do at the local level. When you talk
    about 'empowerment' and 'vulnerability'...these terms
    weren't even in my vocabulary...'feminist' wasn't either. I
    didn't know I was a feminist until I read Betty Friedan's
    book *The Feminine Mystique* (W.W. Norton, 1983), when I
    was in my late sixties...then I had an explosion of con-
    sciousness. Now, my career itself, which essentially didn't
    start until I was sixty, has empowered me in many ways, and
    given me a platform, if you will, to do for myself—but also
    the power to do what I can for other women. I could have
    been just as successful if I had managed a farm, but I was in
    politics. It was all accidental."

    Mary Louise continues: "I appreciate that some women
    of our generation feel their identity is linked to that of their
    husbands' so that the loss of a spouse heightens their inse-
    curity and contributes to the void, making them feel power-
    less, invisible, and the like. But for many, widowhood has
    an empowering aspect. Now, Elmer died in 1980, and I did
    not have a difficult time at that point in my life, except for a
    normal kind of grieving. I had my career and he had his; he
    was a physician, but he was in medical politics. So there
    was a place where our interests converged. He empowered
    me, and I think I empowered him. He encouraged me, he
    supported me, and he was very proud of me throughout my
    career. I think that widowhood—this doesn't sound right
    the way it comes out—offers a kind of freedom, a freedom
    to do things the way your instincts were telling you to do
    them all along. My widowhood coincided with my leaving

the organizational aspects of my political career. The two together gave me the freedom and independence to expand my horizons, to speak for myself—things that I would not have otherwise been able to do.

"Looking back, another thing that I believe had to do with my empowerment was the fact that during World War II, for a period of five years, I had the sole responsibility for rearing three children and total responsibility for family management. I'm sure it was empowering, although I did it because I had to do it.

"Now, I not only go to seminars, but I sometimes speak about aging, new beginnings, starting over, or something like that. I start over every day. I just don't think of myself as old. Sometimes I walk in a mall where I look at myself in the big windows and see my reflection and think, 'Who's *that?*'"

GWEN: "That happens to almost every woman you ask. It's so consistent, the way people are shocked by the physical change they see—because they don't feel it."

MARY LOUISE: "I don't know whether I look like I'm seventy-eight or not. People say 'You look *young!*' Well, I don't get excited one way or the other. I think I probably look exactly the way I *ought* to look at my age!"

ELLIE puts the wrap on the subject of taking control of one's life by reading us a list of the factors she feels either empower or describe empowerment for the New Older Woman:

1. Circumstances are such that we are taking charge. "We weren't wearing the pants to begin with, but things happened and taking control was legitimized, and it didn't worry the man."
2. Having your own separate money, or account, or some sort of control over a portion of the money, so you can choose to do anything you wish with it.

3. Being financially secure means having the ability to devote professional energies to volunteer work.
4. Being free of old stigmas regarding social patterns of marriage, such as being a widow, being unmarried, or being divorced.
5. Being able to have a space of time without obligations of family, after children are grown and before one might have to care for aging parents.
6. Having strong female role models in one's family or strong mentor relationships of some kind.
7. Having personal space—a "room of one's own."
8. Having time to pursue personal interests or enter a new profession.

JUDITH: "I would add, *overcoming adversity or depression* as an empowering factor. You can grow and develop as a result of real trauma."

ELLIE: "I also want to add one more thing to the list: *confident, self-assured husbands—men strong enough to allow women the freedom to develop.*"

GWEN: "Older women seem to take more control of their lives than older men. Men retire and wind down, while women look forward to doing more. Women continue growing and become more powerful; men don't make the transition with the same vigor."

### SEXUALITY AND MENOPAUSE

*"Are we saying that older women and sexuality don't go together? Of course not!"*

Despite the openness with which we are discussing our lives, loves, careers, successes, and disappointments, there is an unexpected reticence to discuss sexuality and personal intimacy. We circle it for a bit, talking about the lack of significant rituals in our culture to mark the passages from childhood into adolescence, and from the mid-years into old age. And we muse on the significance of the terms used to describe these passages. When we were in our girlhood, the words "menstruation" and "menses," and later, "menopause," were mysterious, ominous. (We noted and were curious why they all started with *men*.) The term from our adolescence, "the curse," was more straightforward. For the present passage, "the change" is, by comparison, a gentler term. Finally, Gail voices what is missing:

GAIL: "I jotted down a few things that I don't even think we've more than touched on indirectly, and they're noticeable in their absence: sex and sexuality. Are we saying that older women and sexuality don't go together? Of *course* not!" Carefully, the conversation unfolds.

JUDITH, who is bringing her organizational bent to our often rambling thoughts by compiling notes for a profile of the New Older Woman, says she is adding the entry: "… *comfortable with emotions and ideas, but not comfortable talking about sex.*"

ELLIE: "It *is* giving us pause: women are not comfortable talking about money *or* sex."

JANE: "Sex is wishful thinking with many of the older women I've talked with…sex simply isn't that important to them."

GINNY: "Is this an avoidance issue?"

MARILYN: "It's important that it doesn't become another taboo. …We've talked about menopause, but we didn't really talk about sexuality in our fifties and over—we keep skirting around that one. I think one of the aspects of growing older, in my case at any rate, is that the sexual drive is not as powerful as it used to be. So instead of fantasizing sex, I fantasize massages…I lie there and think, 'Now what could be the most wonderful thing that could happen to my body?'… and I think of massages."

GINNY:  "There was a film called *Eating* (by Henry Jaglom, 1991, producer, Judith Wolinsky, released by International Rainbow), about women's relationships to food. In it one woman said, 'Oh, I wish I could meet a man who interests me as much as a baked potato!'"

MARILYN:  "When I was in my late forties, I asked an older friend whether she'd been through menopause. She replied, 'Yes, and it wasn't such a big deal,' then added, '...and my sex life got much better!' In fact, she said she had the beginning of a great love affair at the age of forty-nine. I was touched by that; it helped me to get over the fears that I was having at that stage. Mind you, I'd been in women's organizations for fifteen years and no one had ever mentioned that subject in a personal way before!"

GAIL:  "Here's what I hear from women I've interviewed in their fifties, when they talk about previous stages of their lives. When going from pre-puberty into early adolescence, they describe suddenly becoming vulnerable....Hollywood describes it as something wonderful...but the reality for most of them was something else. These are powerful women in powerful positions, and they describe the period of adolescence as a time of realization...a time when violation and pregnancy become possibilities. There are all these associations that are still so vivid in their minds that in their fifties they recall this as being synonymous with what it was like becoming an adolescent female woman. It also extends to the whole area of anger (which in so many women is repressed or diverted in very nasty ways), and to finding acceptable channels for aggression....

  "I think there's an interesting link between being in one's fifties and pre-puberty: that girl we left behind before the sex role and before getting scared about saying what we really thought in front of boys...when it was all right to be climbing trees and having adventures."

HARRIETT: "I empathized with Gail's thoughts on the strangeness of adolescence. We all *do* recall the discomfort with our bodies; we weren't sure what was happening. And then there were the changes in our relationship with boys...the pressures from without to please them. Our values somehow depended on how well young men related to us... which in that sense, takes away one's power."

JUDITH: "The women I interviewed for my book *Choice Years: Health, Happiness and Beauty Through Menopause and Beyond,* (with Pamela Gordon; Villard Books, 1991) were all in their sixties; they said they had a lot of sexual desire after menopause, and to the degree that they were sexually active, they had good sexual relationships...but they just weren't looking for it. And about 25 percent said they were enjoying a new interest in sex; a new-found freedom."

JUDY: "...*and,* free of the burden of possible pregnancy and problems with menstruation!"

JUDITH: "Women have male hormones too, and after menopause their bodies stop producing them; what provides women with libido is testosterone. Men's testosterone levels diminish much more gradually than women's. Testosterone replacement therapy under clinical supervision is now being chosen by some women who have experienced a lack of desire—and it works! It doesn't change your sexual relationship, or heighten desire; it's simply like having your body returned to you."

ILENE: "Does it produce facial hair?"

JUDITH: "Well, yes, there's some increase, so you have to adjust dosage levels. There are also cardiovascular side effects to this therapy, which are also a factor, so one has to balance the need versus the risk. At the time I started the therapy, I wasn't looking for a surge of energy...I was just experiencing a certain *aridness* in looking to the future. Sexuality in older women is a neglected subject. We don't see older people portrayed as sexually active in magazines or films. I think it's a very well-kept secret, how many women are now marrying—or having relationships with much younger men. This is a true story of a ninety-year-old woman I met in a nursing home. She'd married young and been divorced in 1910, tried a second marriage that didn't work, then entered a long-term, passionate relationship with a younger man. It was the joy of her life, and ended only when she had a stroke. When I asked how much younger the man was, she replied, 'By now, he'd be about forty.'"

CECELIA: "When I was interviewing older women for my graduate work, the professor on my master's degree program committee said, 'You can't interview them and not ask them about *sex*.' So with the very first woman I interviewed, I started by saying, 'I'm shy about asking this question, but some people believe that women in their seventies and eighties are not interested in sex. Could you tell me how you feel about it?' She replied, 'I wouldn't ask that question if I were you.' And I thought, 'Oh God, I've really put my foot in it.' There was a long silence. Then she said, 'This is how it is for me: I've become a vegetarian, but every once in a while I want a piece of red meat. And I go out and get it, and eat it, and enjoy it!' This is the way it was put to me, and I accepted it as an answer, so I put down on my questionnaire, 'Some interest in sex occasionally.'"

SALLY: "Some women simply don't have a choice: there's no partner, and they have to accept it if they're at an age when they're not interested in another relationship. When I was younger, I felt insecure, unpopular, if I didn't have a man. Now, when I don't have one in my life, I'm very grateful that the testosterone has disappeared. I'm comfortable without a man."

MARY LOUISE concurred: "I get along fine…I have no problem whatsoever. There *are* moments of loneliness…but we mustn't equate solitude with loneliness. I *like* solitude, I like to be alone—I like hours of it. But there are times when you simply need and want to interact with people, with no thought of sex."

SALLY is rather wistful: "I notice, as a widow, that it isn't only loneliness...one would like to be the *first* in somebody's life. I miss that."

MARY LOUISE: "I would be the first to say that being seventy-three or seventy-eight doesn't rule out the possibility that you can have another relationship—I see a lot of them. There's a lot of companionship in a late relationship...but I don't know how sexual it might be."

CATHERINE: "There are people who are worried about their lack of interest in sex as they get older, and there are also those who may feel abnormal because they're still interested...because they grew up in a society that assumed sex ended at forty."

JANE speaks from her own research: " My chapter on sexuality in *Growing Older, Getting Better*, (Addison-Wesley, 1983) was the hardest I ever wrote. I tore up reams of paper, and I finally concluded that what women really need is intimacy: to be hugged, touched, stroked. Intercourse? Of course, if it happens, okay...but that's not what we *need*: We *need* intimacy. There are very few options for intimacy for older women, and they need it. We should do more touching of each other. I think it's as important as any other facet of life for us after fifty."

GINNY: "In a research project that I was associated with at the University of Southern California, a major problem that emerged was the great loss of human touch as you lose a partner, especially if you don't have children that you have that kind of contact with...and how women who live together are frowned upon and assumed to be lesbians simply because they live together. And so women sublimate their feelings and go into the closet in regard to this wanting to reach out and to touch. That's the value of 'pet therapy,' as it's now being called, where intimate association with live animals has been shown to have theraputic value for older patients. This business of hugging and being touched and being looked in the eye is part of the sexuality of aging and is a great loss to many older people, men and women alike...because they don't have a companion. I know there have been some terrible scandals in nursing homes...like, an older man creeping into an older woman's bed at night...and the family being called the next day and coming and taking Mother away from this terrible place. Of course, Mother loved it!"

CECELIA: "My research confirms these observations. Most of the women I interviewed did *not* define sex exclusively in terms of intercourse. They referred to touching, hugging, kissing...loving to cuddle. On the other hand, several of the subjects claimed active and satisfying sex lives—often, as a result of having shared mutual pleasures and interests such as travel, sports activities, gardening, or music."

ELLIE: "Has anyone done any research on alternate forms of non-Western sex? There are traditional ways that women handle these matters in other societies, such as in Oriental and other cultures, where women don't just 'accept'; there *are* alternatives."

CATHERINE: "You know, I was struck by the discussion in *Ourselves Growing Older–Women Aging with Knowledge and Power* (Simon & Schuster, 1987) of sexuality in the later years and of 'pleasuring one's self.' The advice was that if a woman were going to do that, she should spend the whole evening building up to it by playing music, taking a warm bath, lighting a candle, romancing herself a little bit. I think there is a lot more need for *context*...for creating an atmosphere of relaxation and affection. And it was striking, in that for women there has to be some atmosphere of warmth and desire."

MARILYN: "Well, what is certainly clear is that the sexual drive that was so strong in adolescence and young womanhood, it didn't take very much to get to a point where you needed the release. But at this stage of life, it takes a little more. It's not going to happen unless you attend to it in a different way."

RUTH ASAWA introduces an artist's variation on the theme of sexual pleasures. "Sometimes I'm so excited about a little painting I'm doing that I'll work through the night. I think it probably happens to people who write, or people who do other creative things. What I would like to call that is 'beyond sex.' I would like it to excite young people. There's a lot more than drugs, sex, and rock and roll. You can experience incredible excitement from something like a science project or a music performance! And so I would like to get the idea of that kind of excitement across to schools. Children need to experience and know that there are alternatives to going to bed with someone."

VIRGINIA reminds us of historical taboos on discussing both menstruation and menopause. "In the Victorian era, as Marilyn wrote in her chapter for, *Victorian Women: A Documentary Account of Women's Lives in Nineteenth Century, England, France and the United States* (Stanford University Press, 1981), "menopause marked women as reproductively useless, no longer 'sexy.' A century ago some women didn't experience menopause because they died before it happened. The survivors didn't even talk to each other about it. Many had heard dreadful tales of unpredictable and heavy bleeding and feeling a little 'crazy' (from hormonal swings) and terrible night sweats. Young women picked up bits and pieces of this information and dreaded the onset of menopause. Doctors, being male, had no personal experience of the wild ride of menopause and generally considered these complaints to be neurotic and not to be taken seriously."

GAIL: "Could we take a poll around the room? Did you or did you not have any difficulty with menopause and did you or did you not take hormones?"

Her question evokes the almost unanimous response that menopause was relatively easy for most of us, (with some of our older participants admitting to having forgotten what it had been like, or even at what age it had occurred). A generational attitude may have contributed to this lack of emphasis.

RUTH B.: "I don't remember women talking about it."

CATHERINE: "For an earlier generation it was the great 'bogie' — this terrible thing that was going to make you insane..."

PAT: "It coincided with my most productive period. I was a full-time mother, a full-time teacher creating a new program curriculum, and I had a husband in a public position who needed my support...."

MILDRED: "That was my situation also...just too busy to think about anything else."

BETTE: "We weren't having vapors on the couch. I know that."

Almost all the participants were, or had been, on some form of hormone therapy, which research indicates is successful in preventing osteoporosis (bone loss) and has been reported to reduce heart disease by a phenomenal 50 percent. Ilene reports she has been on estrogen since the age of thirty-seven as a result of a complete hysterectomy, and has always felt it contributed to her good health and high energy in the years since.

JUDITH: "The percentage of women in this room who are on

hormone therapy is not typical. In the general population, only 30 percent of women take hormones. Even when recommended by gynecologists, they're not taking them. Women have an enormous fear and suspicion of the medical community and of the drug community. Most prescriptions are never filled. The actual percentage was around 10 percent when I started research on menopause — it's somewhat larger now. But the prejudice against hormones is intense. The studies are 'in progress,' but if you're in menopause, you need the answers now. And when you're talking about maintaining good health in order to enjoy your later years you have to make decisions based on what is known now. The decision women have to make is which risk to take. Taking no hormones, for instance, doing nothing, leaves you at high risk for heart disease and osteoporosis. As Jane Brodie said in the New York Times, 'Women would rather make an error of omission than commission.'"

ELLIE: "The only thing cited by doctors, however, is that you might get osteoporosis and that your husband will push you around in a wheel chair. I went in for a bone-density test when they said, 'If you don't take it, your bones will self-destruct...whatever...' And I must tell you what was left on my answering machine by the doctor: 'I just want to tell you, Dr. Zuckerman, that you are deteriorating at a normal rate!'"

MARILYN: "I think it's important for young women to realize that the menopausal period goes on for several years."

GWEN: "I think it's a real error to say menopause is a breeze. Some women do *not* go through it easily. It is estimated that 25 percent of women have a rough time of it, and I believe that — because I was one of them. I could have used some advance information. I had always felt simply, 'menopause...what's that?' I didn't even think about it."

DENISE: "I need to compare notes with other women because I can't find information from the scientific world. I asked my doctor and my gynecologist—both men—about menopause and they said, 'We don't have answers to your questions.' 'Is it common to lose one's sexuality?' I asked. They said, 'We don't know.' So I said, 'There must be something like that going on because they let women out of *purdah* in Eastern countries after menopause, so it must mean they don't have as much sexual feeling.' And the doctor said, 'You're way ahead of me, kiddo.' And even the feelings that I'm feeling—I don't know if they're common or unusual, but maybe that doesn't matter...."

GAIL: "I think it does, yes!"

DENISE: "Without my permission, my whole way of being a sexual person changed, and I miss it and I wish it could be another way—the way it was. But I would be happy to find out other ways. I mean, aging people still have sex lives and they're still valuable, and there could be more than one form of sexuality as you grow older. But I can't find out information about that, and what most strongly concerns me is that what doctors call 'secondary sexual characteristics' change too, by which I mean my emotional life. It's almost as if I see my life, now, as a stage set: take away the props and things change. So I don't feel the same emotionally. I love my husband, but it seems to be a different kind of love, which isn't really what I wanted."

GAIL: "Is it the desire for sex? Because that seems to be the chief change in sexual response."

DENISE: "I have less desire, and I don't like that; I like it the way it was. But they say, 'Well, these things happen and different people react differently...' You don't get more than that. You don't get a sense of what to expect *next*. Will it come back after menopause? It seems not."

GAIL: "Did you discuss hormones at all?"

DENISE: "I'm on estrogen. I agree with the approach my doctor takes; he seems very careful."

GAIL: "So you take estrogen and progesterone?"

DENISE: "No, just estrogen. My doctor recommended this. *Ourselves Growing Older* suggests that, given the present evidence, taking progesterone is not necessarily the best approach, but my doctor and I are watching the research."

GAIL: "Doctors don't have the answers. The answers don't exist because there haven't been any long-range studies. Probably a majority of women don't fill—or don't continue taking—their hormone prescriptions the way they were prescribed. The main reason is because of Provera, the 'false progesterone.' Many women go off the Provera and just take the estrogen without telling their doctors, largely because it doesn't do what they expect it to do in easing the discomforts of postmenopausal syndrome. So they're really on estrogen replacement and not on the combination. The combination of progesterone with estrogen is supposed to reduce the chances of developing endometrial cancer from 4 percent to 0.3 percent."

MARILYN: "The word 'replacement' has a lot of meaning. With replacement therapy—that's what most of us are doing in terms of estrogen—we're starting a period in life in which certain things that we've taken for granted, that have come naturally, have to be *replaced* by others."

CATHERINE: "We are talking about sex—the reduction of the sex drive and the fact that the sex drive withers in many marriages as if it were a personal loss. But I think you also have to think about a continuing sexual relationship as one of the things that makes this whole very difficult enterprise of marriage possible…and it then leads in very important ways to the kinds of caring that are likely eventually to be necessary between two people.

"If you look at human sexuality and the sexuality of other

mammals, the big difference is the detachment of human sexuality from the fertility cycle. What was the selective advantage for human beings of being able to enjoy sex that could not possibly lead to reproduction?

"To me, the only logical answer is bonding: in the sense of keeping two parents available for the rearing of children—bonding because of the tremendous commitment involved in reproduction by women. Then there's the bonding that has to do with care of each other as you get older. The sexual relationship makes caring for someone a loving enterprise."

MARILYN links the two chains of thought: "I like the word 're-placement' because there is the assumption that, even if something gets lost, there is something to take its place."

## HUSBANDS AND PARTNERS

*"Women seem to take more control of their lives than men; men retire and wind down…women look forward to doing more…"*

In spite of the travails we experience in negotiating the tricky currents of the menopausal passage, postmenopausal years offer a potential for greater sexual freedom—assuming there's a still an active healthy partner ready and able to share them.

The promised vision is indeed attractive. With prospects of recapturing another decade or more of prime time, women look to their partners for shared company as they enter a new phase of life. Free from the responsibilities and concerns of younger years, they visualize a new kind of active, fulfilling companionship exploring individual or shared interests, "striding happily down the path of life, hand-in-hand, into the sunset…." The reality is often somewhat less rosy.

Most of us still lead active professional lives and relish them. All but a few have husbands who are semi- or permanently retired. The unexpected problems created by this situation are reported as ranging from the rather absurd to the seriously disruptive; nearly all cast a pall over those sunny later-life expectations.

The most common complaints are about the irrational, domineering, and competitive behavior of newly retired house-husbands. Many of us speak resentfully of having our time and turf usurped by aggressively territorial mates: "By the time I retired, he'd already staked out the territory: the house, the phones, the kitchen," says one woman. Others note the loss not only of space and privacy, but attempts on the part of the spouse to take over their friends and interests.

SALLY, now a widow, remembers: "He had nothing to do, but wouldn't accept suggestions. He seemed determined to show me he wouldn't do it *my* way: 'Don't tell ME what to do!' But when I retired, he wanted nothing to do with me—that would be an admission of weakness."

JANE: "The first year, he wouldn't plan one thing; he became dependent upon me. It was terrible. Then he went back to school…he was excited: the new lessons, the people of all ages. But, I wrote all his papers. Maybe you call that being an enabler—but I was trying to be an enabler for happiness. I never thought about it, but, I think he was competing with me. When I went back to school and got my Ph.D., his colleagues would ask him how it felt to have a doctor for a wife. Maybe that sort of jibing from his peers did it, but after that there was real competition that had never existed earlier."

Some women noted that when the retired husband is ill or inactive, problems are compounded.

MARY LOUISE remembers: "My husband—he was an M.D.—

worked up to a year before he became ill, then came home to die. I came back from my job in Washington, D.C., and handled as well as I could the anger that came into our relationship for the first time. He tended to do bad things so someone would have to give him extra attention...then he would be angry at being dependent. And there was his resentment of my good health, my vigor. I was confused by his irrational behavior, and mine."

ELLIE: "This is a very important conflict, because there are a lot of other things we could do if we didn't have to worry about and pity the other person. Anger is the only emotion allowed to men, but denied to women."

SALLY: "After they retire, men experience a lack of ego satisfaction—a loss of power in their loss of work—while women have a whole range of activities to choose from, and have multiple demands on their time."

GWEN: "Most women have automatic networking skills, and are also more likely to have multiple roles. They have greater curiosity and a willingness to try new things while keeping old roles: church, family, friends. Their most common adjustment in retirement is to keep something from their personal archives to carry over with them."

LIBBY: "After my husband and I retired and moved to the Bay Area, my son encouraged me to try Transcendental Meditation. He introduced me to a guru in Berkeley, who taught me my private mantra to chant, and swore me to secrecy (mantras must never be given away). My husband became *obsessed* with learning it! I resisted, he persisted, then insisted: 'If you love me, give me your mantra!' He kept at it, and finally, in great turmoil, I shouted it at him and ran out. Later, in tears, I told the guru what had happened. He asked to hear my mantra, listened, and then said, 'But, you don't have it quite right' and gave it to me again...so I still had my mantra! Later on, my husband tried meditating himself, but found he didn't have time for it."

MILDRED speaks fondly of her spouse: "I'm preparing to depart on an expedition to the headwaters of the Amazon soon. He gets a little upset when I leave, but he's accepted it for our whole married life, which is sixty-one years now, so he's quite used to it."

For a last word, we are indebted to the Japanese, who have a term for the man who hangs around the house, sticking close to his wife: *nureha*. It means, literally, "wet leaves." So, our Private Woman strides into her new life-stage, adjusting to changes, and following her heart—doing her best to envision a productive future, and, if need be, wiping the old wet leaves off her shoes.

# CHAPTER THREE

# The Outer Woman

"Confidence," "self-esteem," "feeling good about yourself" —
from children to adults, the nineties have immersed us in
courses, workshops, and seminars aimed at bolstering personal and professional self-confidence. For those old enough
to remember Dale Carnegie's popular 1950s book and mail-
order course, *How to Win Friends and Influence People*,
today's search for inner identity and outer packaging has a
"we've heard it all before" echo in our group's circle of
friends.

Not only is the older American woman challenged by ge-
netic, environmental, economic, and social influences, but
also by media portrayals, fashion trends, and no-end-in-sight
options for cosmetic surgery. Though the nineties have
pushed hard at relaxing the boundaries, one constant clings:
America is stuck in a youth mode that devalues women over
fifty. Studies show that this moment of truth comes ten years
later for men. Thirty-five and forty-year-old women find they
are less employable with each passing year, especially in the
corporate sphere. Fear of losing jobs to younger workers
forces them to work longer for less pay, to try harder, and to
stay young-looking and radiant in the process.

The old saw that beauty and brains don't come in one package has enjoyed a long run. It stems from the historical role of women as decorative sex objects whose gifts were cultivated and maintained primarily to bolster male self-esteem. Those ladies weren't expected (or advised) to burden themselves with intellectual baggage. Things have changed: being bright and beautiful has been in vogue and highly marketable for a number of years. But being bright, beautiful *and young* opens the doors of today.

Along the way, the New Older Woman may have chosen to utilize every tool of fashion, cosmetics, and medical science to wrap the goods, or she may have opted for a more casual, "natural beauty" regimen, but whatever her approach, the deeper wrinkles, body sags, and thinning hair bring reality home. Her comfort level is shaped by years of habit, her individual outlook dictates choices.

What is *not* available to her is a wide range of choices.

As we settle in for another discussion after a healthy lunch of lentils and yogurt—where the fitness and radiance of guests fresh from the hot baths, massage, or spiritually uplifting experiences is on parade—the subject of image, fashion, and beauty options takes on heightened interest. Our own images and exteriors, as well as how the rest of the world sees us, are up for a reality check.

We suggest there might be something to be learned from the *Lear's* story. While it was in publication from 1988 to 1994, this magazine tried to develop a more mature readership, presumably to include older women. Who was "the woman who wasn't born yesterday" as *Lear's* subtitle put it?

BETTE: "Always thin, always beautiful..."

DENISE: "And rich enough to buy what's advertised..."

BETTE: "The first couple of times I looked at *Lear's*, the clothes were all size four or six, a jacket for the working woman was

$1,700, and the skirt hems reached the upper thigh...hard to see how the *mature* woman could possibly bend over the files or do anything else...."

CATHERINE: "Their market was pretty narrow: wealthy older women. You had to have money to be interested in reading it and there was a huge distortion of reality, but no greater than the distortion of *Seventeen*, which I used to read at that age; it had models with impossible legs and impossible waistlines and impossible complexions. Those images didn't correspond to reality and *Lear's* was about as real for the fifty-year-old woman as *Seventeen* was for the average teenage girl."

PEGGY: "When *Lear's* first came out I wrote to Frances Lear several times objecting to the dichotomy she displayed. She said she talked about the experienced older woman. But her models were twenty-five...or never over thirty. I got some rather nasty replies. One said she didn't want to hear about the women fifty and sixty. 'I don't need to discuss it because age should be irrelevant: But if you don't like it, don't put the pressure on *me*, go to the advertisers. Go where it will have an impact.' In other words, she wasn't listening, but she was urging me to make my influence felt. I felt it was a rather testy letter, but what she said was true: money controlled her output. She had no choice."

DENISE: "*Ms.* magazine showed Russian women on the cover without makeup and they lost an important cosmetics account."

JUDITH: "When I broke into modeling at age forty-seven, my first job was for hospital pajamas, but I was happy to work! They had me in a rocking chair in this long step-in robe that completely covers you. Then I did a job for *Lear's* magazine. I was photographed nude from the hips up, with my arms crossed over my breasts. Now, when I put the two images together, it points out there's a major confusion out there about just *who* older women are. They don't know what to do with them. It's easier to end up ignoring them."

LIBBY: "Fashion houses *are* confused about what message they should be putting out. Maybe that's changing, though, because recently a friend told me that a top American designer wanted to start using older models and asked if she could send him my picture. I said, 'Sure.' She told me the answer was that they didn't think I looked matronly enough! I was rejected, so I don't know what they're looking for."

ELLIE: "I don't believe there's the least bit of confusion. The *Lear's* premise *does* have a message and it's that youth equals visibility and acceptance. It reminds me of that image of the young woman entertaining the troops during World War II: thousands of soldiers with all eyes on her. That equals personal power—power you get from being young and sexy. That's why it's hard to give up youth. Our society doesn't have any wise, mature position for us to move on to, there's nothing defined and ready for us, and that's why we have to make it for ourselves—*change the playing field*, make our own new definition."

JUDITH: "*Lear's* tried to use older women at first and they started a fad for a while, a new market trend. I'd go to a modeling session and be surrounded by six-foot-tall, one hundred-pound, gorgeous twenty-year-old women. In the middle of all that my gray hair stood out. Photographers, everyone, became excited: "Younger women are a dime a dozen... hey, look at this, we have something new, something interesting!' *Lear's* started the fad, but it soon faded."

PEGGY: "I asked students to analyze *Lear's* women. With feature stories about mid-life women and photos of younger ones, it was a mixed message, they said. But, predictably, it was the visual image of the younger women that made the more dominant, lasting impression."

VIRGINIA: "Society is aging, but magazines like *Cosmopolitan* and *Ladies' Home Journal* are still going strong. Both focus on younger women."

PAT: "*Vogue* magazine is doing the same thing. They used to have elegant clothes for mature women and feature well-known, distinctive older women like Katherine Hepburn, Georgia O'Keefe, Lauren Bacall. They haven't done anything like that for a long time."

DENISE: "One magazine does write about older women: W. They write about their achievements. They write about rich old women. But on balance, they're pretty good; their profiles are succinctly written and often very interesting."

IRENE: "In the first issue of the revived *Ms.* magazine, Gloria Steinem summarized the problem of advertising, the imposition of advertising on editorial decisions; the new *Ms.* has no advertising. It's a great magazine now."

CECELIA: "*Modern Maturity,* the largest-circulation magazine in America, has gone a little overboard in its effort to get rid of the stereotypes of aging: the wheelchairs, crutches, incontinency, and all that sort of stuff. What you see is people golfing, taking world cruises, hiking, cooking wonderfully healthy foods. They don't want to give readers the downside of aging at all. Actually, they don't want to give the reality of aging."

CATHERINE: "So what we're hearing is that publications aimed at the mature audience are not able to present an image of older people that is positive without being deceptive."

JANE: "They may carry stories about older people, but their ads show very attractive, usually younger, mid-aged people. They reinforce the concept that power and vigor is represented by youth."

JUDITH: "It's recently been proposed that advertising is the chief means of communication in our culture today. It elects presidents and from there on down it influences how the world sees us within the power structure....it should be monitored. Image is everything."

## ECCENTRICITY

*"I became 60 last week, and I'm no longer going to pussy-foot around!"*

There's a particular brand of confidence that women acquire over the years—a self assurance built on having logged over half a century of intellectual growth. It's a confidence that opens the doors of previously closeted taboos. It puts one in the "I don't give a damn what anyone thinks" mode, and has no patience for circling a subject with polite, time-consuming niceties. The room becomes a circle of nods whenever the subject is mentioned. We admire the daring called eccentricity; we're comfortable with directness; we're enjoying our status. We feel we've earned the right to be blunt.

DENISE: "A young Italian friend who's an architect and a feminist laughed when an American male who went to the beach with her in Italy couldn't look at her and wouldn't go near her because she was topless. She thought that very, very funny. I said, 'Well, I personally prefer to keep my nudity private,' and she replied, 'But Denise, we're not talking about *you* because you're too old.' And so I said, 'Carolina, what would be wrong with my being nude on the beach?' She said, 'No, no Denise. You couldn't *possibly* do that!'"

MARILYN: "Have you ever seen the Brecht movie called *The Shameless Older Woman*? It became my model. It's a marvelous French film about a woman in her seventies whose husband dies and all the children are expecting that she'll settle down and wear black and give all of her belongings to them. Instead she takes up with a group of socialist Bohemians who run her about all over the place in their car. Of course, she spends money on them. Her children are absolutely outraged. But you know, it's a growing view, this sense that women cannot be eccentric until they become widows or until they manage to stop thinking about what others will think."

CATHERINE: "I think eccentricity is an interesting issue. *I've* always wanted to be Bella Abzug."

BETTE: "I recently went to a management seminar called "Situational Leadership" as part of my job and, while I subscribe to the fact that there's always something to learn, at the end of it I was asked, 'Now what do you think of *that?*' So I replied, 'For forty years I've been going to management conferences and the words are new but I've certainly heard them all before.' My answer was considered outrageous and eccentric and something that only *I* could get away with because I was old!"

DENISE: "Do you think if you were a man you would have still been considered eccentric?"

BETTE: "Probably not."

DENISE: "I think using the word eccentric in that way is a put-down."

BETTE: "Oh, I do too. In some cases it is."

CATHERINE: "But the line between being a slightly eccentric older woman and being a dotty old lady is a very thin line. Eccentric includes anybody who is non-conformist, but it's also applied to conspicuous women in general. The norms of behavior are such that if you move a little this way or a little that way, it's 'uh-oh!' But come on. Being eccentric is one of the pluses."

BETTE: "A colleague who just reached sixty was never as irreverent as I have always been, and at a recent meeting I noticed a change in her behavior. She usually said what came to mind, but in a diplomatic way. All of a sudden she came out with an absolutely outrageous statement without softening it in any way and I was completely taken aback. She then announced to the meeting as a whole, 'I became sixty last week and I am no longer going to pussy-foot around. I am going to say exactly what comes to my mind!'"

## BEAUTY

*"Less whistles—is that what we're talking about?"*

The saying that "beauty is only skin deep" is in for an airing as we warm up to the subject of the New Older Woman's facade—the part of her being the world sees first. Naomi Wolfe's *The Beauty Myth* depicts the confusion of accomplished women who feel emotionally and physically tortured by the need to look like movie stars. Does the quandary dissolve or accelerate by the time fifty and sixty roll around?

Joining this morning's conversation, Esalen program director, Nancy Kaye Lunney, says there's a flip-side to the proverbial "ugly duckling" legend in her experience. She's just turned fifty-one and is feeling good about it. "When I was young, I never thought of myself as pretty and attractive, so I don't have that thing about getting older because I'm not losing anything, like, 'Oh my God, it's going.' I feel I'm getting *better* and it's nice. I see a lot of women who are getting older and who are terrified because they've so identified with a certain kind of prettiness and they can see it going."

CATHERINE: "One of the things that's certainly true of me is that I like my gray hair because of the state of mind my mother was in when her hair was turning like this. She looked pretty to me and therefore having my hair turn makes *me* feel pretty. And I'm enjoying wearing more grays and silvers; it's an interesting 'high' for me. But the point is that this attitude is available to me because the image was available to me."

MILDRED: "My mother had this beautiful white hair and I just couldn't wait to look like her and was very annoyed that I was about sixty before I had any gray hair."

PAT: "I think sometimes the saddest woman in old age is the one who was the raving beauty when she was young and learned to depend on that for attention; then, when her looks fade, she doesn't have anything to fall back on. Then it's, 'Oh my God, the only attention I ever had was because of my beauty…what now?' A lot of movie stars go through that kind of thing."

JUDITH: "Less whistles—is that what we're talking about? Actually, age can be an advantage in some circumstances when you don't want to be an attraction."

GWEN: "I'd like to talk a little bit about *wrinkles*. OK, that's the crux of it: those little lines that grow deeper each year are major players in the beauty dilemma. Maybe there are some things you can do about them if you really want to be radical, but most of us live with it. In a recent study young people were asked what they looked for when assessing people's age and most said wrinkles, hair, and skin tone, in that order. How can we re-cast that? What do we do with the societal image versus our own reality?"

JUDY: "Why are we defining ourselves so much by biological factors and how we look?"

GWEN: "That's what this discussion is all about. You can say, 'Who cares,' but look in the mirror: happy or unhappy?"

SALLY: "I have a valuable suggestion: see that your mirror is against a window."

MARILYN: "I really feel that each woman needs to design herself. It was easier for me when I was younger to take the position, 'Oh no…no eye lifts, no facelifts, no skin peels. I'll never dye my hair.' Well, I dye my hair. That was the first change. It came a few years back and I'm comfortable with that. And every time I try to let it grow out, I see all of the gray and white, and I just don't want to be gray-white. So now I have to reappraise how I feel about some of these other interventions. I have a friend who had been gorgeous when she was younger and as she got older her face began to sag and fall and one day she came to a reception we had at Stanford and she was suddenly gorgeous again. She made no bones about it and said, 'I had my face lifted and if anybody wants to know who did it for me, I will be more than happy to tell you.' And she added, 'I was very unhappy when people stopped looking at me and now everybody turns around.' And she's remarried. So I am reassessing my own views about what women, individual women, are willing to do for their looks. I don't have a totally negative attitude anymore. I get a lot of flack from some of my feminist friends when I say that openly."

ILENE: "Women who don't use cosmetics, hair dyes, or other enhancements are just as consciously choosing a 'look' as those who do. They're sometimes a bit smug, or intolerant, as you suggest. Is that another kind of denial?"

MARILYN: "Possibly. In some feminist circles, the beauty cult has been considered a dirty word—looked down upon. In *The Beauty Myth*, which I reviewed for *The Washington Post*, Naomi Wolfe portrays the beauty business as a billion-dollar industry that's become a religion. There *is* a lot of evangelical fervor in the weight-loss movement. But the fervor of those who are intolerant or disdainful of women who use available 'enhancements' becomes part of a pretty passionate platform too."

GINNY: "Can we come back to the point again that it's good for some women and it's not appropriate for others? I guess growing old gracefully can be redefined by every woman in this room, but I feel not making a woman feel guilty about keeping her gray hair or about dying it is important. It's her body and she can do as she darned well pleases about it. I have many people ask, 'Ginny, why don't you dye your hair; you'd look much younger.' I just say, 'You can do what you want to, and I'll do the same.'"

RUTH B.: "I tried dying my hair for a while and I just got bored with it. It's just too much trouble."

DENISE: "When my mother let her hair go gray, the color complemented her skin tone beautifully and she looked marvelous. It's the way it was meant to be. Just pretty. Now she dyes her hair again. It's a kind of walnut color, but the last time she went to a salon outside Geneva to get just the right color, they had forgotten to order it for her. So my mother met me at the opening of the National Gallery with bright orange hair."

PAT: "Your mother is doing it for her own personal pleasure, but for a woman to try to remain youthful all her life because she's depended upon adulation or because it's her only positive feedback is pretty pathetic because you can't do it forever."

ELLIE: "I think a certain amount of narcissism is actually a very good thing, very healthy. It's serving my mother in good stead because she pays very good attention to her body; she gets massages, she watches every little thing. Sick people don't take care of themselves until they begin to feel better, then they pay attention to grooming again. That's a healthy kind of vanity."

ILENE: "In California, Palm Springs is one of the celebrity centers for cosmetic surgery. A friend who can't abide this talk about 'should I or shouldn't I?' asserts that there's nothing to argue about. When she makes her routine visits to Palm Springs, she calls it 'just good maintenance'—as sensible as servicing your Rolls Royce. She says her body is more valuable to her than a Rolls."

SALLY: "Our image should not be that of the twenty-one-year-old, but I'll compete with anyone here on vanity; we're probably all vain to some degree. We want to be looking the best for our own age."

JUDITH: "Yes. We don't want what I call the 'whatever happened to Baby Jane' look."

PAT: "Could we agree there are two views of this issue: that it's okay to use 'intervention techniques' as Marilyn calls them, if you're doing them for your own personal contentment, but that it's wrong for a woman to do these things because she thinks that other people will value her more?"

BETTE: "It depends on what business you're in. I have a friend who was a television anchor for CBS and when she had her fortieth birthday party she also renegotiated her contract to include facelifts and other cosmetic procedures. In her contract! She has subsequently lost her job because she was too old. Last weekend I ran into another well-known, once-popular television anchor woman—she's just lost her job and she's in her fifties. It depends on what you do."

PAT: "Denise, you have such a child-like, fragile beauty, do you find that men in your firm look at you and think, 'Oh, she's such a little girl, we can't take her seriously?'"

DENISE: "If I was that little girl, I would be treated lovingly and tenderly, which I'm *not*."

PAT: "But you're a very naughty little girl because you fight back."

DENISE: "I'm seen as a witch! When people say 'congratulations on the award to your husband (architect Robert Venturi),' I say, 'I thank you on the part of my husband, and when I get one myself, I'll thank you for myself.' They are horrified by this. I mean, how can I be so immodest and pushy?"

PAT: "If you looked different, you might be better able to get away with it."

DENISE: "If I looked like Greta Garbo."

MARILYN: "In *The Beauty Myth*, Naomi Wolf dubs the 'PBQ'—Professional Beauty Qualification—as a necessity for women in any kind of public business. And it's an appearance standard that is not only expected of you if you are in television, but more and more in all types of business positions."

PEGGY:  "We don't require this of men. It's not fair. "

BETTE:  "She's not saying it's fair. She's just saying it's what happens."

DENISE:  "I'm not so sure we don't require it in men. I've known men who have developed bunions from the kinds of dress shoes they wear, and they have to wear dark suits for important meetings. I think there is a demand on men. Also the tall men that look like Vikings get the jobs. We've got a marvelous cartoon on our wall at our office; it came from *The New Yorker*. It's an advertising agency and down the middle of the corridor walk two executives. Left and right are two teams of male workers. From the left, they point out, 'Here is our design *image* team,' who are obviously all Harvard grads, wearing tweeds, smoking pipes, their hair combed back, and six-foot-three. And the other says, 'Here is our design team,' and they're small, scrawny, hunched up, frustrated, with their hair all over the place. I think image is very much the situation for men."

IRENE:  "It's *not* only a female dilemma. Men have it too: whether to wear earrings, whether to let their hair grow, and if so, how long. For job interviews they're told they have to take off their earrings. I agree; they have societal pressures about external appearances, too."

CATHERINE:  "But it's not linked with age in the same way."

DENISE:  "Well, I sometimes ask young architects in our firm, 'Couldn't you grow a beard or something so you'd look older?' because some clients won't trust our project managers if they look too young."

RUTH B.:  "It's very clear that some men in television have had facelifts. And I'm sure they do it because it's important to their job—stopping the clock in order to look the same from year to year."

JUDY:  "It's extremely difficult for women who are in front of the television camera every day to stay on top. The implication is that they can't possibly do their job or be interesting communicators if they don't look the part, and right now the part goes to the younger woman."

PAT: "Women are in a double bind. Men begin to lock us out when we fade. They can age with power intact. We can't."

JUDY: "Women will not get power through externals. You get it through achieving in your chosen work. At the heart of it is the ability to choose work and use talents to the fullest. This is not exclusive to women. If you're going to make a difference in practical terms, you have to talk about what happens to older women in the market place."

GWEN: "Not all women are in the marketplace. What about women who opted to do other things?"

LIBBY: "I understand what Judy is saying: whatever brings joy to your life, whatever you feel defines you, is worthwhile. You should be judged on that and not superficial outside or sexual appearances. Nobody worries about Eudora Welty's wrinkles. Now that I'm living back in my hometown, people say 'Wow, you look terrific!' That's great, but I want to say, 'That's not all. I'm interesting; I have things to talk about.' I want to be admired more for what I can do than what I look like."

ELLIE: "You have to *make* yourself visible. So how do you do that? Here's an example: I could have said I was coming here to talk to a lot of wonderful leaders or to sort out my priorities, but I said, 'I'm going to a *think tank*,' and people thought that was very important. Impression management is a part of beauty."

JUDY: "I don't think you can change one's image just by these external things or even by new language or new dynamics."

IRENE: "You can. It has already taken place. In the sixties, the women's movement changed the way women were portrayed in children's books. That was a constructive contribution that involved simply instituting a new language.

Patriarchy is not dying tomorrow. In modern movies like *Thelma and Louise,* we see heroines who are powerful and villainous. These are types of pressures that have changed images of women. It's not a stretch to suggest it could happen for older women also. There are all kinds of pressures; political pressure is only one piece of it. Maybe what we need is some sort of renaissance. It may be happening. What really bothers me is that I hear people here buying into the beauty myth."

ELLIE: "We can't reject the beauty myth simply because it's the only power given to women. There's a part of this youth and beauty concept that we *want*—for *ourselves.* We exercise to keep up our vitality. We take pleasure in putting clothes together, selecting colors and textures to achieve an esthetic. We want the vitality, energy, enthusiasm, and excitement that's associated with youth, but we have to select the kind of youthfulness we want: extract the good part, throw out the idea that we exist for someone else. We have to find it for ourselves. The press isn't going to find it for us."

JUDITH: "But does it have to be either/or? I think our whole conversation is something of a dilemma. We went so far with the discussion of appearance, then all of a sudden we said, 'No! No! No! Don't judge me by what you see outside—it's *inside* that I'm beautiful.' There's some denial in that. There's something inside every woman that says her appearance is very much a part of her intrinsic self. It's the part that helps cancer patients regain their sense of themselves through showing them how to use makeup, wigs, and so forth. I think it's denial to assume that women write appearance away easily and say, 'Oh, the heck with *that.*' There's a struggle in there, and some anger. I myself feel this. I see myself as beautiful and yet no one even looks at me in the street!"

PEGGY: "They did a comparison of two television people of

comparable age, Dan Rather and Barbara Walters, and the comments came back that Dan Rather seemed rather *young* to replace Walter Cronkite, and that Barbara Walters was '*still hanging on.*'"

PAT: "But do we want the New Older Woman to think she still has to look young?"

CATHERINE: "There's a whole industry out there investing in making the New Older Woman spend money to look young. Without condemning the individuals who make that choice, I think the question is, what can we do to make the other choice more rewarding and meaningful."

RUTH B.: "I think if we're all intensely interested in what we're doing and if we're being very creative we don't think so much about how we look. We want to look reasonably respectable. But we certainly don't care about going to extraordinary measures."

BETTE: "We don't have time, either."

VIRGINIA: "What you remember about a person is not the wonderful makeup, the great hairdo, the clothes, but the way one's eyes show enthusiasm and vitality—the flexibility and youthfulness of their minds, not their faces."

DENISE: "I also get a lot of joy out of facial structure, and that shows more as you get older—the bone structure."

VIRGINIA: "Left alone, the skin of many older women develops an extraordinary translucency and beauty. It's the kind of beauty that's only earned by having invested many years."

### THE OUTER WRAP: BODY DILEMMAS

*"You want something that gives you a little shape, but hides the bulges."*

PAT: "Another problem for the new older woman is fighting the fashion wars. When you arrive at a mature age and full figure, the clothing designers and manufacturers don't make anything that looks decent past a size twelve, possibly a fourteen. Since there are going to be more and more of us, maybe we need to make some direct appeals to the market to make clothes that really work for us."

BETTE: "We need to influence and pressure the retail marketing system. I'm tired of going into stores and finding what in my childhood were called 'frumpy frocks'; now it applies to clothing for older women. They hang straight down and they're usually made of that horrible crepe that is so God-awful that it makes me shiver—pale lavender or pale blue or pale rose. Choices that wipe me out completely. I keep trying, and I ask, 'Why don't you have a size sixteen; why is everything size four and eight; why do you stop at fourteen?'"

MARILYN: "You also have a problem if you're a small older person. I look through petite-size clothes but they're styled so you end up looking like you're trying to be sweet sixteen, cute, or preppie. There's not much that's elegant in petite sizes."

CATHERINE: "It's pretty bad in larger sizes too. Lane Bryant is a real downer. But there's a store in New York called The Forgotten Woman that's terrific. Those of us who live in college towns where every store caters to eighteen-year-olds envy those of you who live in retirement communities like Carmel."

BETTE: "I had a very interesting encounter in a little suburban boutique where I now buy nearly all my clothes because when I'm on the road it's difficult to shop. It's a small store and they don't have a lot of room for things, but the owner recently said, 'You know this is unbelievable. I can't keep my size sixteens in the store and I've noticed that my most loyal customers are the size sixteens.' I said, 'Well, of course, because there's no place else to go for them.' She's doing a landslide business at the top end of the size market and is only occasionally selling a four, six, or eight."

DENISE: "There *are* stores that carry designer clothes for older women, but you spend $1,000 for a jacket. In France there are good middle-class ladies' working clothes. But they don't send these styles to America. You have to go to France to find them."

RUTH A.: "What kind of clothes do older women prefer?"

BETTE: "The same kind of clothes as younger women."

RUTH A.: "Loose? Suits? I really don't know because I'm not into that."

DENISE: "Most women in business need a suit and, of course, you're bulging in different places and you want something that doesn't make you look like a box, gives you a little shape, but also hides the bulges. Those are hard to find. When I was in London, I noticed that Mrs. Thatcher wore marvelous suits and I asked where they came from. Everyone in England seemed to know that she got her suits from Aquascutum; you could ask anyone and they knew. So I went to Aquascutum and said, 'I want a Mrs. Thatcher suit.' And they said, 'We can't help you. We make them specially for her.' But they're just the right thing. She's sort of big and they make a nice little shape, they're not overdone, and she looks like a lady—just what you'd want. The problem with mass-producing things like that is that each woman has slightly different bulges."

MARILYN: "Has anyone had to look for a mother-of-the-bride dress? They are so bad…peach, lime-green. They're either so dull, as if they came out of a fifties movie—or they're weirdly asymmetrical, the skirt is way up on one side or there's a flower tucked down there and ruffles over the top."

PAT: "I think they're purposely made to add ten years."

VIRGINIA: "Part of the solution to this problem is to find your own style—what feels good to you—and then find a dressmaker. There are still good dressmakers."

BETTE: "That's expensive. I have all my skirts made because I can't find the right fit. And it's also very time-consuming."

PAT: "But the point is, we shouldn't *have* to find a dressmaker. We should be able to find clothes on the rack just as we did when we were younger."

MARILYN: "I think what needs to be clarified is that this age group has its own parameters, its own characteristics, its own beauty. We're all saying that no one is addressing this stage of life. The cosmetic and plastic surgery industry is telling us that we have to look younger while the indifference of the clothing industry offers the choice of looking older or younger, no middle ground. If we had a wish-list of things that might come about as a result of this conference, one would be that the fashion industry pay attention to women from their fifties through their eighties in a way that's appropriate to their age. They have to think about what it is that enhances our beauty rather than trying to make us into something we're not."

## YOU'RE AS OLD AS YOU FEEL, AS OLD AS YOU SAY

*"I have to remind myself that I'm not the contemporary of my daughter's friends."*

None of us *feels* old. Yet inner feelings and outer reality are often in conflict. The anxiety level for one woman escalates with each new wrinkle, while another is comfortable with whatever Mother Nature deals. The differing attitudes give rise to equally mixed messages in advertising, the media, and in our own perceptions of age.

PAT: "My *Lear's* story is about who comprises the market. When I received the complimentary first issue with the request 'Would you please comment on how you feel about the magazine,' I felt it was a hoax. I wrote back my thoughts and I got a letter that explained, 'Well, you must understand that women in your age group tend to think of themselves as being fifteen years younger. Therefore, we are projecting this magazine fifteen years under your age.' I'm paraphrasing, but that's generally what Frances Lear's letter said."

CATHERINE: "Could we explore what that means? Because I know there's a sense in which it's true and several of us in this room have said it. When we're with younger people, for instance, we feel as if they're age-mates. I have to remind myself that I am not the contemporary of my daughter's friends. So that's certainly a sense in which I think of myself as younger than I am. It could mean a lot of things. I'm not sure what it means."

DENISE: "Gloria Steinem said that no one knows what a forty-year-old woman looks like because no woman will admit to being forty."

PEGGY: "I used to get very angry with my mother because she always spilled coffee on her driver's license, to hide her birth date so she could take off some years, and she got away with it for a long time. When I was young, I thought this was very vain and was arrogant about it. Looking back, I'd like to be able to apologize to my mother because she was a working woman and that was a necessity for her, but at the time, I thought it was vanity."

DENISE: "My mother says a woman who will tell her age will tell anything. I discovered her age when I was about twenty because the census forms she filled out had been returned for some reason; originally, she had waited for everyone to leave the house before completing and sending them in so no one would see her age. Then the bureau sent the forms back, and she was exposed. I've always told my correct age."

GINNY: "It's interesting at what point you start *bragging* about your age."

MARILYN: "That's the way I feel about my marriage. For years, I didn't tell people I how long I'd been married because I felt like a period piece. It seemed tacky to be married to the same person for so long. No, really, don't laugh. Now I feel like something of a phenomenon and so I'm happy to tell them now."

ILENE: "This conversation is interesting when you remember how we felt as teenagers. Most of us couldn't wait to be older and added a year or more as early as possible in order to rush being grown-up and sophisticated—with all the excitement and privileges that implied. Now I know a seventy-year-old woman who is giving her age as seventy-five, sometimes eighty, and she revels in the response, 'You look so *young* for your age!' So I've been thinking, here we go again—hiking up our age—and it's at the other end of the life span!"

## THE LANGUAGE OF BEAUTY

*"When someone is trying to be particularly complimentary, they introduce you as a 'young lady' when you're obviously an old lady!"*

We're in agreement with the old adage: "It's not what you say, it's the way you say it." We bristle at phrases like "the blue hair crowd," "little old ladies in tennis shoes," "golden oldies," and other condescending euphemisms, so what would we prefer?

JUDITH: "We were talking earlier about language. I was looking at photos of older women recently and saw a new mysterious sensuality and beauty in them. A new language is needed to define this so it's not just a poor imitation of the younger image."

GWEN: "When someone is trying to be particularly gracious or to compliment you, they introduce you as a 'young lady' when you're obviously an old lady; it's uncomfortable, even though well-intended. In Ruth Jacob's book, *Be An Outrageous Older Woman*, (Knowledge, Ideas and Trends, 1994) there is a poem that says: 'Don't call me a young woman; it's not a compliment or courtesy, but rather a grating discourtesy. Being old is a hard-won achievement and not something to be brushed aside, treated as infirmity or ugliness or apologized away...I am an old woman, a long liver. I'm proud of it...I revel in it.'"

GWEN: "It might be a good idea to find images of sensual older people and make a big deal of them, support the people who choose to use them. A phone company used an older couple in an ad and they were so beautiful, and I think Kodak has done this also."

IRENE: "Give those companies awards. It's a popular thing to do these days, and it can be effective if you're a group with political recognition."

GWEN: "The Grey Panthers used to give lemon awards in medicine."

[The Grey Panthers are a Washington, D.C., consciousness-raising action group that focuses on issues that affect the quality of life for older adults. The Lemon Awards cited samples of shortcomings and failures of the medical profession to adequately or properly address specific health problems.]

JANE: "The organizations that could spearhead action are having problems keeping their heads above water, except AARP, which is successful because it has a strong lobbying force. Passion is what's needed to keep groups like the Older Women's League (OWL), and the Grey Panthers going, and it's usually the people with passion who guide them and bring them into being and who are responsible for their success. When they move on, things change. Look at what Maggie Kuhn has done for the Grey Panthers and she's still out there at age eighty-six. At a conference in New York recently, she had to be escorted across the stage—she couldn't have made it on her own—but for forty-five minutes she gave this impassioned speech that turned everybody on.

And many, many of the people in the audience were young."

PEGGY: "The baby boomers will be coming along, and I think they'll do something about it. They won't let themselves be labeled. Judy, do you think the media is ready to talk about this coming wave of soon-to-be older women facing the facts of aging? Does it hold any interest in the world of documentaries or feature stories?"

CLAIRE: "What about *deserving* to be recognized?"

JUDY: "That's a good word...but I think the media wouldn't be interested in a story about the baby-boomer generation impacting the market, though they might do a story about older women who are interesting, who have accomplished something, or about something specific in a single older person's life. That's the way people who cook up stories think.

"My own view is that the media would do a story on Claire, or Mary Louise, not because they are older women, but because of what they've done in life. The issue becomes defined in terms of the story."

ELLIE: "That's precisely what we want. I'm sure if an older woman wanted to talk about her passionate Parisian love life at age eighty, it would get attention."

JANE: "I think there is an audience for the airing of older women's issues and it would include a lot of younger women who may be apprehensive. They'd see that growing old isn't so bad. The question is how do you go about changing media attitudes about this kind of programming?"

MARY LOUISE: "I see two different tracks. Judy says our real image is what we are inside, what we've accomplished. I have never felt rejected or invisible, but we're complaining about how we as older women are presented in the media. We have every right to resent some of the images: bladder-control products, false-teeth cements, and so on. The public doesn't really want to see us as role models or images for selling other kinds of products in the commercial mainstream."

As the meeting breaks up, Claire asks Mary Louise if she will sit for some sketches this afternoon. "You have a beautiful face," she exclaims, "I've been wanting to draw you ever since we met!"

# CHAPTER FOUR

# The Transition Years

The bonus years her generation has inherited have arrived and are looking her squarely in the face. She may or may not be ready to take a hand in shaping the way they will bring her maximum satisfaction within the framework of family, friends, and society. She may not even be aware of the slippage of time; a life's accumulation of deferred plans may still be beckoning. But she *does* have a greater range of choices than her counterparts of the past and if she's healthy and secure financially, her options are limited only by her interests. Or *are* they?

Some new things are happening: adult kids are returning to the nest; longer lifespans increase the odds that she'll spend some of those bonus years as a caregiver to elderly parents. The burden of maintaining the nest for the longer haul may force her to seek alternative housing options. And if that's not enough, society may be asking more of her as community agencies turn increasingly to volunteers for providing needed services.

We decide to devote a session to talking about this process of transition and the myriad factors that will influence what we hope will be 'prime time'—the 'option years'—for the New Older Woman.

JANE: "There are more transitions for women in their middle years than at any time in their lives. Each woman thinks she's going crazy with her own set of transitions, whether it be divorce, going back to school, or whatever…they can be very good transitions, but they're *there*, and they crowd in on you. We need to be aware of this, so that women can prepare… or at least know they're not alone."

PEGGY: "One thing that strikes me in Cecelia's study of vital women in their seventies, eighties, and nineties, is that they all mention the art of 'letting go' of certain things gracefully —so that they can hang onto others. They have a real sense of priority, wisdom.…"

CECELIA: "What they actually 'let go' was the ego. Ego gets in the way of all kinds of things in one's life, and these women were nonconformists…highly individual."

BETTE: "We seem to be encouraging people to live in the present…to live each day to the fullest but concentrate on the present, not a year from now or five years from now, but the present moment."

DENISE: "How do you plan for old age and live in the present?"

RUTH B.: "Well, I think you have some overall plan, but you don't think of it too much. You just think about how marvelous the present day is…how marvelous what you're doing is. But way in the back of your mind you know you have some kind of plot for the future, but it's not an overwhelming concern."

CECELIA: "When it came to planning for the rest of their lives, the women I studied wanted to stay in their own homes, and they told their children that even if it involved having help, they had everything all arranged and taken care of financially."

BETTE: "Did you get a sense of the fact that, since these people had already planned what their life would be for the future, this was a big help in their enjoying the present? Because

sometimes when there is order in your life—for some people but not for everybody—you are better able to enjoy the
present because you've taken care of those things which are
no longer hanging over your head."

DENISE: "...and this is why we talk about planning: making those
decisions for the future and therefore, freeing yourself up to
enjoy the present."

## HOUSING ISSUES: WHERE IS "HOME"?

*"Communities should offer options for old people—to live
singly, downtown, in the suburbs, with family, in a group—
that's the challenge."*

We agree that underlying later-life planning is the security
of the place called home. Coming in all sizes and locations, its character is shaped by personal circumstances and
preferences, and certainly limited or expanded by the pocket-
book. In studies conducted by such organizations as AARP,
older people express a predilection for remaining in their
own homes, independent of anyone else—especially when
or if they become divorced or widowed.

Denise, whose career in urban planning and architecture
has challenged her to tackle the question of satisfactory solutions to housing options for all segments of society, feels
that each situation has its own criteria.

DENISE: "You're all concerned about housing and I feel you expect I have these wonderful ideas about how women can
live in the future. I'm a bit skeptical because there isn't any
set formula. There are social questions, physical questions,
zoning requirements, personal preferences. All impact architectural decisions."

CATHERINE: "This is more a city-planning question than an
architecture question. Most housing in this country has

been designed for the model nuclear family. What's been built recently is not well-designed for people living alone, or for people living as roommates in an egalitarian manner. For instance, if you look at recently built apartments, they all have an obvious master bedroom…public and private space is not designed for adults who are living together but not necessarily sharing the same bed. It's not designed for people who have parents living with them. And in a sense it's not well-designed for people living at home who have health problems; and it's certainly not designed for people who can't drive!"

GINNY: "There's a political issue here, and that's zoning restrictions."

DENISE: "I think zoning is one of the major means that America uses to achieve apartheid. It doesn't have to use such draconian measures to achieve it as South Africa did."

MARILYN: "I question why all housing in this country *is* made for the nuclear family model. Why haven't some enterprising architects and developers designed houses that are intended for two or four single adults, a couple, or a mother and a child in which there might be four bedrooms and some central living space with a kitchen and living room. And I know this goes counter to the whole American ethos of individuality, but when I see all these women living in their apartments in Miami Beach, most of them widowed, it's sad. The idea that maybe two of them could share in some way seems to be anathema."

The answer, Denise says flatly, is money—and zoning. "If people have the money, the market *does* respond. You can see it in the housing for the wealthy elderly, like the Del Webb Corporation's Sun Cities in California and the Southwest, which are planned communities for people fifty-five and over. They're profitable for developers and they meet housing needs for those who can afford them."

BETTE: "There's another phenomenon coming to pass right now that's going to escalate in the future. It's older persons living in suburbia, isolated because they can't drive anymore, hidden away in houses they're holding onto because it's their only major asset."

DENISE: "My theory is that a housing strategy for a city or a region should be very complex and should allow all sorts of different opportunities. There should be 'sunshine cities' for people who want to live that way, opportunities for those who want to live with their families as well as for those who don't...old people who want to live downtown, and those who want to live in the suburbs. Single people who want to rent in the suburbs should be able to, and various types of group housing should be available. The idea is to find a way to help as many different housing arrangements as possible happen. A lot of them can't happen without changes in zoning. I'm interested in zoning as a tool because it has built into it the possibility of waiver. There have been lots of court decisions, lots of precedents that severely restrict what can be built or what can be done with existing buildings. Zoning is so sensitive to community pressure, it's called a 'weak reed,' because it bends in the tide. But I feel that's right; when these social changes happen, zoning should eventually give way."

Denise adds that, "When older people *do* want to live together in communities, they can find a suitable mix of housing in old residential neighborhoods in cities. Large old Victorian houses get converted into fraternity houses, or housing for the elderly. They could also be converted on a neighborhood basis to more than just the housing. But it's very difficult to do that when people don't have confidence in the city."

GWEN maintains that, "Many elderly people really *like* retirement homes. In other countries, notably Canada and Scandinavia, successful models exist."

DENISE: "You may be horrified by 'sunshine cities,' but many older people prefer that semi-communal life style."

JANE, whose book *Living Longer, Living Better* (Crossroad, 1991), identifies model housing ideas for older people here and abroad, notes that, "In Scandinavia, where there's been co-housing for some time, a beautiful cyclical thing happens: generations help each other naturally and lovingly. And more and more I think people will want to share intergenerational lives. Economically it makes sense. 'Put two people living in poverty together and you can afford to buy something.' Does it really work? In co-housing there's usually a high turnover at first. But when things settle down—when the group finds it's truly compatible—turnover decreases. Over time, there's very little turnover; strong interaction holds the group together."

BETTE: "What's going on now in the Washington, D.C. area is that they're building a lot of apartments that have an entry hall, a living room, a dining room, two master bedrooms, two bathrooms, and two dens. And that's because in Washington you have lots of single people sharing, and not all of them want to share the same rooms. So somebody is beginning to think about that, fortunately."

JANE: "That's why I wrote my book, to let people know that there *are* ways...to let them know that if they don't wish to live alone, they can live with several people or one person. I'm not talking about the frail or elderly, or 'Where do you put Mom?', but where do we put *ourselves* so as not to be alone, unless, of course, we choose it. I attend conferences on affordable housing and there's very little talk about zoning and privacy, very little talk about housing for older people who want community and privacy. There's very little ingenuity on the part of architects, either."

GWEN: "Some folks prefer age-segregated housing. They say, 'I've raised my kids; I don't want to worry about anyone, about tricycles underfoot or babies crying.' They want to be safe, secure, and free to travel. These people feel that being creative reduces loneliness, and that it's not so bad to be segregated. The problem is for low-income people; you need a lot of money for most new model ideas."

DENISE feels there is no lack of innovative, imaginative, and potentially successful solutions for a range of housing needs, but reiterates the fact that none can be realistically enacted without substantial investment, significant changes in zoning, and a national commitment. Wonderful designs for living for older Americans are out there, if the government and its taxpayers are willing to help pay for them. "In America a lot of people, the majority of people, have housing that more or less suits them and they don't care about the ones who don't, so you can never get housing to be a majority issue. Also, because we see our metropolitan areas as a set of little towns that support themselves, we can't establish a metropolitan tax base. Try for it and you're called a socialist. We should be looking for the mechanisms that will give the widest help, but at this point we don't even have the creativity to think through which would *be* the best mechanisms."

CATHERINE: "I don't want to miss something else Denise said while we are talking about housing concepts. We should notice that some of the projects have a time sequence built in, which is to say you have one kind of living at one level of health and you have already made provision for access to the next level of care that you may need... and there may be a progression of four different ways of living out one's later years. I've thought about getting together to live with a group of women, but you still have to say, 'What are we going to do when we need the next level of care?' And it's these transitions from one level to the next that become so traumatic for people. There are often waiting lists. You solve one problem and the next one is upon you. It requires a lot of investigation and planning."

The uncertainties of alternative housing are not present for the reported majority of women who prefer to remain in their own homes, but other realities limit or impinge on their lives. The spouse retires and household arrangements come under his scrutiny and control (often resulting in the woman feeling resentment, anger, or guilt at the usurpation of her privacy). Or, a new phenomenon of our generation occurs—the kids come home.

LIBBY, in her soft Texas drawl, speaks to the topic: "We have an old family saying about children: 'Out of the nest by twenty'. Now, they're in distress and we get them back; or they want financial help. It's a real problem!"

JANE: "It's a *very* big problem. Just when we thought we were all alone, after raising all those kids, six months later someone came home. At first I didn't resent it, but I thought, 'Oh my God!' It's a revolving-door policy—I guess it's called 'rewarming the nest'—and it's probably happening more and more. And part of the problem is jobs...."

BETTE: "Yes, a single parent or even *both* parents coming back, with children! They've lost their jobs, or can't afford to pay rent...."

ELLIE: "When I grew up, there was no shortage of jobs; there were plenty out there."

JANE: "Our generation never thought of going home again, no matter how hard the going was. This *is* a new phenomenon!"

GWEN: "It was Robert Frost, I believe, who said, 'Home is where, when you have to go, they have to take you in.' But it's probably happening later and later now, with all the divorces, low birth rates, the economy, whatever. We had a revolving-door policy for the kids: all five left and came back at one time or another. There's one at home now and really in crisis. And he resents it because it's so difficult to come back to 'Dad's house.'"

BETTE: "This new phenomenon, or at least the new *quantified* phenomenon of unlaunched children coming back home to live, comprises, according to a recent article I read, 19 percent of eighteen-to thirty-four-year-olds."

LIBBY: "They just want you to put the money in a tree stump in the dark of night so nobody knows where it comes from!"

GAIL: "That was one of the items on a list I was making of things that might help to prepare for this older stage. One should be able *not* to be sucked back into being the caregiver again, particularly the laundress and bed-maker, for a perfectly capable male child of twenty!"

GINNY points out that for older people the reverse option is also not always acceptable: "That is, many older people don't *want* to move in with their adult children, either. On the more positive side, here's a statistic that speaks to the housing situation for the elderly: 80 percent of the over-sixty-five population own their homes, mortgage-free."

BETTE: "One housing option for older single women who wish to remain in their own homes is the reverse mortgage. If you own your home outright, or have so much equity in it that you're close to burning the mortgage, the reverse mortgage gives you money to live on for the rest of your life on a pre-fixed basis and the house becomes the property of the bank, or the money paid out becomes a lien against your equity. It's a mechanism that encourages older people to remain in their homes—they can't throw you out. The downside is that it diminishes the value of your estate…less to pass on to heirs."

HARRIETT: "The reason it's called 'reverse' is that normally you pay the bank; in this case they make *you* a monthly payment which comes out of the equity in your house to give you cash at a time when you're cash-poor but house-rich. There are mixed things about this, of course. It solves one problem, but in terms of the whole society, it takes away the normal turnover or transfer of property which is more likely to be at a price that younger people can afford. And it leaves an older woman holding onto a house that's often larger than she needs."

The implications of trends in housing for older people, and the incidence of the "back-to-the-nest" migration of adult children, interface with another area of increasing concern: caregiving and caretaking.

## CAREGIVING: PAINFUL RESPONSIBILITIES

*"It's important that we talk about caregiving in a way that doesn't make it debilitating."*

Except possibly for sex, no subject arouses more emotion in our group than that of caregiving and caretaking. Whether this is because of pain, guilt, pity, or perhaps because it induces a whiff of our own mortality and strikes close to home, we are reticent to deal with the issue. Yet we agree that it's one that is, or will be, an increasing part of life for the New Older Woman—and an even larger reality for our daughters *and* sons.

GINNY: "It comes down to actualities of caregiving and how one balances life after some of the realities hit you with a two-by-four. How can you be new and old at the same time? What kind of role-model do you establish for the daughters and daughters-in-law who are coming along afterwards? Where does responsibility begin? What happens to the new freedom, new potential, new opportunities we've been talking about when we have to face the realities of caretaking?"

PAT suggests going around the circle, asking each of us for one word or phrase that expresses an immediate reaction to the issue, prioritizing what each of us feels to be our most important concern. The responses are delivered in staccato phrases and are frequently contradictory, ranging all over the map:

"Sharing the burden—early care intervention—
bartering—paying for every service you get—
avoiding that!—anticipating our own needs in
terms of someone else's—caring is an outgrowth
of love; if it's not an expression of love then
don't do it!—guilt—resentment comes into it—
balance!—balance in terms of your loyalty to
the caregiver versus your own—time, energy,
money, self-care—making it a national policy
issue—family support—bad timing—no time—
there's never an appropriate time for a caregiver—
intergenerational caregiving—phased-caregiving
—assertiveness with medical practitioners—
from the personal to the political—
organizing and focusing resources—financing—
share-giving as well as care-giving—dependents,
interdependence, and independence—
what about co-dependents?—skills in crisis
management—skills in care —appropriate
equipment for care—information on care—
adaptive technology and innovations—
education for caregiving."

MARILYN perceives a hidden agenda of a political and sexist nature: "There's a whole literature on caregiving and whether
it's a women's issue."

PEGGY: "How about changing the perceptions that it's *just* a
woman's issue?"

BETTE: "That's what I was saying, that's what I was meaning:
*Don't* always make it a women's issue! There's a study being
done now funded by the Andrus Foundation at the University of Southern California, and it shows that there are an
increasing number of male spouses taking care of females,
especially among people who are dealing with Alzheimer's
disease."

GAIL: "Societal caregiving is one of the possible goals or objectives to which women can look forward as they approach getting older. But will that be attractive to the baby-boom generation of women who are approaching fifty now? It's tied up with the concept we mentioned earlier: that you grow up thinking you should give something back. It's also tied up with religious upbringing, civic upbringing, parents and role models to whom service was an integral part of life. That seems to be one of the main things that's being lost in this country."

CATHERINE: "I think we're talking about different kinds of caregiving. There are the issues of women who have to recycle personal caregiving, becoming grandmothers who are the babysitters of their grandchildren: that's one kind of issue. Another kind are the women who go through a cycle of personal caregiving and then generalize that into some kind of societal caregiving. And then we have the issue that, on the one hand, we're concerned with people who in their older years may be unable to care for themselves, or need social support. And at the same time, we have the negative throttle of people who invest all their care in themselves throughout the life cycle, in the kind of selfish hedonism that's being associated with the baby-boom generation."

GINNY: "What bothers me about caregiving is that when you're giving to a person, you take away their control, you take away their independence; whereas care *support* means that they're part of the team."

DENISE: "On the other hand, the caregiver *needs* support."

GWEN concurs: "It's important that we talk about caregiving skills in a way that doesn't make it debilitating. People who find themselves in caretaking positions need to know there's help for them. There are a lot of women in that place now, and they've had no training, no preparation."

BETTE, speaking from her AARP experience, is blunt: "When

we tried to get volunteers organized to give respite care to caregivers (going into a household for a couple of hours and giving the caregiver a little break), it didn't work. And we finally figured out that people felt, 'There, but for the grace of God, go I—and I don't want to deal with it!'"

CATHERINE: "There are many cultures in which it's understood that children care for their parents to pay their parents back for caring for them. That has *not* been the major theme in American culture. Here, you care for your children to pay your parents back for caring for you. There's reciprocity, but it's a recycling reciprocity, as an investment in their care for *you*. Now, we've gone through a period when we've believed that with the development of Social Security, it should be possible for adults to save enough so that they will not be dependent on their children. We're coming up on a point where the whole notion of socializing the care of the elderly is breaking down, and we're realizing we're not able to do it."

HARRIETT: "The older woman reaches her fifties and maybe is at a point where she should really be talking about a period of opportunity; then she becomes a grandmother, and it's a temptation to take that on and deny herself the opportunity to be defining herself in different ways. So what I'm saying basically is, don't get put in that caretaker role... and I think that with social and economic changes and the cost of day care and women working, it's a problem we have to look at."

BETTE: "Seventy-five percent of nursing home residents are women, and a bunch of them don't belong there, because they either just outlived their families or their families lived far away. And there's another issue that just surfaced recently, about sick old people being dumped at emergency rooms and just left there...."

RUTH B. enters this gloomy colloquy like a ray of sunshine. She admits unabashedly to a lifelong passion for helping out and doing good. She is a true caretaker, dedicated to service, to the community, and to people. "I keep getting these ideas about things that we just absolutely need to do! I'm energized by my inner feelings, and I don't ever see myself stopping. Project Open Hand, that now serves a thousand meals a day to AIDS patients in the San Francisco Bay Area, just grew exponentially, and somehow or other things we needed always came. Miracles would come along, like when we needed about a quarter of a million dollars to buy a building...I just go on my way and have this connection. Lao Tzu says that planning one's future is like trying to take the master carpenter's place: if you try to do it, you're going to bang your thumb or something, and it's not going to work...one should simply let the source take over and guide you."

GAIL: "It sounds to me like you're using the feminine principle for all it's worth!"

RUTH B.: "I just feel really compelled to do these things."

GINNY: "I'm experiencing a caregiving role right now. My mother is eighty-three and her health is not good; she's had five heart attacks this year and finally had a pacemaker put in....My husband's into his fourth year with Parkinson's disease, and my daughter was just diagnosed with Grave's disease. So I find myself in a role that many women find themselves in—giving up something that's interesting and exciting in order to be the nurturer and provide the care."

RUTH A.: "I think that the greatest risk a woman takes is the job of parenting. Because you're not just painting nice pictures or making a pot or writing a story, but you are helping to mold individuals who are going to become adults, and then they're going to face old age. I think what you do with your family really influences how you become old...to shape how you then become a child again. Because we're all going to become children again at a certain age, and we have to be cared for by somebody. And you may say you don't want to be cared for by your children, but I *like* the feeling that I've passed on the spiritual lead to my children, and I don't have to worry about the Thanksgiving dinner or the decisions....I'm happy that they make these decisions for me."

CATHERINE: "When your children have grown up, you do, in a new way, own yourself. You belong to yourself. You take a new kind of responsibility for yourself. But I think there is also a very profound intimacy involved in caring for someone who is dying. And until you have that with someone that you have had a sexual relationship with, you don't realize that caring for someone is, at some very deep level, a sexual act."

DENISE: "How about caring for your mother?"

CATHERINE: "I don't think bonding is limited to sexuality, that's not it. Sexuality is only one of the key ways of establishing and sustaining intimacy. Caring for another person is a very profound kind of intimacy. I mean, it's very different when you have to bathe someone and clean them and turn them over, if you do so thinking 'This is a body I love' rather than 'This is a poor withered old body.'"

We all agree that personal caretaking is one of the most difficult and painful of obligations, testing our love and sense of duty even as it forecasts our own eventual frailty. Discussing it openly helps to dispel much of the fear we feel about it. The experiences we share may enable us to meet the inevitable with greater serenity and compassion.

HARRIETT is philosophical: "We're imbibing some values so that by this age, we are much more sensitive to the need for caregiving in the society. We have to keep on learning as society changes, and be ready to modify our own views. And what's part of the wonderful possibilities in caretaking is that it's a two-way street. It's a growth experience in that we continue to grow into it as we grow older."

## VOLUNTEERING: THE GIFT OF SELF

*"Older people who volunteer have a higher level of life-satisfaction..."*

Every woman in the room confides that she'd been called upon at some point in her life to serve volunteer causes, beginning with stints as den mothers, and running the gamut right up to the leadership of powerful non-profit foundations. Without question, doing for others has traditionally been "women's work," we agree. And it's been done willingly, graciously, and competently. The New Older Woman is, by now, a pro. When her nurturing instincts are applied to societal caregiving, everyone is a winner.

GAIL: "I found in doing research for *Pathfinders*, where I draw on a study of sixty thousand Americans for portraits of men and women who have emerged victorious from the predictable crises or accidents of life, that the key—the largest factor of achieving both longevity and vitality—was volunteering or being involved in community activities at some level."

GINNY concurs: "There are three well-documented studies that indicate that older people who volunteer have a higher level of life-satisfaction, a longer life expectancy, and better health than those who are not volunteers—and this means volunteering in its broadest definition."

RUTH B.: "Programs that offer parties and playing are fine from a recreational point of view, but I think older people can do more. They can do things that are more satisfying, that are much more serious and have a much greater impact."

BETTE describes the AARP's volunteer structure: "We have more than 400,000 volunteers across America who work very hard for people who want to do those kind of things. Last year they filled out two million income tax forms for older people for free. We have a program called "Fifty-five Alive" that teaches defensive driving. We run health forums and other forums around the country. In my office we have a women's financial forum for people who are out of the work force. It's run by volunteers and it's in every state but one. We've had women volunteers from age thirty to ninety-six. It's been very rewarding. And we do a program to help women get back into the workforce by building self-image, filling out resumes, and things like that. Our volunteers do just about anything you can think of. They're very, very active and they give many, many hours. The concept of giving back to help others is a win-win situation. As Gail said, it has an invigorating affect on their lives.

"In 1984 we dropped our membership age to fifty (it had been fifty-five) and we now have thirteen million members who are working. Not only that, but every survey we've done shows that a lot of our people who *aren't* working would really love to work. A lot of people leave work at fifty-five; many men leave because of those 'golden hand-shakes'—and a year or two later they're saying, 'Well, this is very nice...but what do I *do*?' We have several hundred volunteers in pre-retirement programs in corporations. Now we're putting together one for women, because what we've found is that the materials available for men don't take into account a lot of the things that happen with women. So, we're redoing all the materials for women."

One of the most significant volunteer roles, according to Mary Louise and Sally, is that of "woman as peacemaker." Mary Louise serves on committees studying international peacekeeping, while Sally is founder of Ploughshares, a non-profit, volunteer, peace-keeping organization based in San Francisco. Both have built strong organizations with volunteer men and women who bring executive and management skills to solving political, social, and global problems.

MARY LOUISE: "Women *have* played a role in peace-making; and they can enlarge that role if we give them some help in mobilizing their skills."

SALLY: "The difference is dramatic when women participate... when they get together, it's powerful. A stunning example of this is the group of women/mothers in Argentina who marched, mobilized, and protested on behalf of lost family members who had disappeared under oppressive military regimes."

# CHAPTER FIVE

# The Political Woman

She arrived at midnight, just nine hours after becoming one of America's most powerful political women. On Sunday afternoon as the first of our forums was about to begin, the National Women's Political Caucus was heading into the 1992 election season. Touted by pundits as "The Year of the Woman," Harriett Woods was elected as its 10th president. Elated, she crossed a continent and negotiated the Big Sur coast to join our discussions.

The next day, the national media tracked her down. All three networks are jousting for the only available phone line, bidding for immediate interviews on their morning news shows. But she resists the temptation. She will provide the yeast for our political brew in the coming hours.

Harriett is a veteran of the political scene, having served as a state senator, as lieutenant governor of Missouri, a twice-defeated U.S. senatorial candidate, a fellow at Harvard's John F. Kennedy School of Government, and a president of the Institute for Policy Leadership. She is also an athlete, her body language spare, taut, and full of energy.

Across the circle of pillows from Harriett sits another political risk-taker and barrier-breaker from inside "The Beltway." Bette Mullen is the director of the Women's

Initiative of the American Association of Retired Persons. She too has an impressive political resume: lobbyist, economic analyst, and the first head of the AARP's Women's Initiative. As director, Bette holds the potential for organizing and leading the largest army of older women in the world, more than nineteen million strong. She offers an intriguing personal contrast, playing "bulldog" to Harriet's "greyhound." Her natural inclination is to keep our dialogue on target, to try to integrate our sometimes random musings into a reasoned whole. She sinks back into her pillows, giving the impression of culling the peripheral and underlining the core issues. When not playing the bulldog, Bette seems the wise old owl.

The two women are seasoned political pros. Raised in a generation of women who were expected to fight political battles from the trenches as good foot soldiers, they have dared to leap into the male-dominated world of political activism.

For most of us in the circle, the "Year of the Woman" has proved illusive, dancing just off the political horizon since Geraldine Ferraro became the first vice-presidential candidate in 1984. It's a tantalizing temptation to take it and run. Like racehorses heading down the homestretch, some of us think we can taste victory, sensing that this time a political surge for women is a sure thing. But we're cautious. So the prospect of women filling political offices this year becomes the background buzz for our dialogue.

## WOMEN'S SENSE OF STYLE

*"I want to see more women in office, not just to change the numbers, but to change the way things are done...."*

We take off confidently with our discussion of women's political potential, but within moments we've hit a predictable snag, the political parallel of the chicken and the egg question. Should we begin by tackling women's feel for power, agenda, and goals, or by examining the unique political style by which women hope to achieve their priorities? Harriett, recognizing that goals and process are inextricably intertwined, opts for linkage.

HARRIETT: "For me, politics is a question of what we're leaving behind. There should be a sense of satisfaction, of impact made. It has to do with changing the way things are, of leaving a legacy. Women bring different values to politics. I want more women in office, not just to change the numbers, but also to change the way things are done. We want to create a world in which all the stakeholders are at the table, where everyone has possibilities for growth, where we care about each other. I've become more and more intrigued by process. I'm more interested in the use of power and how it is applied than in the perception of power. So, even though having more women in government is essential, it's not just getting women elected to the Senate: it's how they use power once they get there."

PAT: "But our public policy still reflects the fact that we don't have enough women there yet...we're not breaking through fast enough."

HARRIETT: "True...there's a glass ceiling. It's like a pyramid of power, a pyramid whose sides get more slippery as you climb. The big gains have been made in the last few decades. Several factors have come together to make it more comfortable for women candidates to step forward and assume the personal risks involved in campaigning. Women are already in place to welcome and mentor, with the blessings of party leaders and women's fundraising organizations like Emily's List. (This is a group dedicated to the belief that women will campaign as successfully as men, given adequate financial resources. The name is an

acronym for "Equal Money Is Like Yeast.") Money, yes—
women can raise as much money as men, but only if they're
incumbents. It's tough on women challengers because they
can't compete for funds. It eats up their energy.

"One barrier just doesn't seem to fall: the perception of
women as less tough, less powerful, less able to deliver.
Many women have to contort their campaigns even to the
point of losing them to prove that they are strong. You saw it
with Gerry Ferraro, you see it in women who run for state
attorney general, you see it when women have to pose with
police officers in their commercials to show they're macho."

GAIL: "A very real stumbling block to moving on up is the 98 percent incumbency rate. Would you be for the Caucus taking
a stand on term limitations as a way of opening up seats?"

HARRIETT: "It's a really tough issue. Probably not. I think that
there are some real downsides to arbitrarily limiting what
the voter does, to summarily ousting someone who might
have genuine talent and who may be working on something with longterm effect. I am hesitant to seek cheap and
easy solutions to what are very deep-seated problems."

Harriett gives us some basics to think about: "The greatest power gains for women have been made at the local
level. We now have more than 20 percent of state legisla-
tors. Two decades ago there were, say, seven female mayors
and now there are more than one hundred and seven
women running the larger cities. These women create a
savvy, experienced reservoir of candidates waiting for open-
ings up the ladder."

Having watched many of their professional friends slip
into a male hairshirt, Bette and Gail seem skeptical that
women can hold on to their working style and still survive.

GAIL: "And as that pool of talent moves on up, what if they feel
they must join the 'old boys' network' to get there and to get

things done? Won't it always be tempting to play the old zero-sum game: 'Go along to get along'?"

BETTE: "Right. George Bush appointed more women to high positions than any previous president, but I wonder what they had to do to stay there."

HARRIETT: "Women have to hold on to the win-win viewpoint they bring to any bargaining table. The point I'm making is that it is also the most effective and economical way to get things done. It creates the most growth for everyone. Ruth Kanter, editor of the *Harvard Business Review* and a prominent economist, gets a lot of money to advise American corporations how to reshape management into a more collegial, feminine style. When women politicians first talked about this, it was considered 'wimpy.' Now that the Japanese are doing it, it's considered smart. Kanter feels we should never apologize for leaving a feminine imprint on the decision-making process."

PEGGY: "Didn't you bring up a movie metaphor over coffee this morning?"

HARRIETT: "*Rambo* is the movie, right? And it became the symbol of the authoritarian, 'beat someone over the head,' male model. So women should take a look at *Driving Miss Daisy*. You all know that story, about a rich woman in Atlanta in the sixties, how her family imposes a black chauffeur on her, and how these two people act with dignity and a sense of self but also with a tremendous gulf between them. The relationship wasn't strong enough; she could not bring herself to invite him to the annual brotherhood dinner. So you have this scene where you hear Martin Luther King's voice in the background, and the camera moves in on Miss Daisy and then pans over to an empty chair. And we see Miss Daisy glance at the chair and in that moment you know that she realizes that she's responsible, that not everybody is sitting at the table. And really, that's what it's all about. We want everybody to be able to sit at the table and speak for themselves. I use these two movies as another way of visualizing what I call *Daisyism* and *Ramboism*, as images of male and female decision-making styles."

VIRGINIA: "Are you saying the male model is inherently victimizing and the female inevitably nurturing?"

HARRIETT: "Exactly. To women, political power should be used as we have used the word 'caregiving' in our conversations. The traditional notion of what power is—standing tall by standing on someone else—is a hierarchical view of politics. To be a victor you have to have a victim. You've got to beat somebody, go bomb Grenada. Women tend to use power to nurture, enlarge, make sure everyone gets a piece of the pie."

PEGGY: "You're good at cutting through the verbiage and helping us visualize complex concepts. Give us a simple, clean image for the mistakes politicians usually make in dividing the public pie."

HARRIETT doesn't even blink. She's ready with a clever, colorful analogy: "There's this story about an orange. A mother walks into the kitchen and her kids are fighting over the orange and she says, 'Stop it. I'll just take a knife…' and she cuts the orange in half and gives each child its' share. The problem is that one of them wanted the rind and one of them wanted the juice. Very often in political bargaining we are afraid to tell one another what our real interests are because we're afraid we'll lose out in the negotiation. I've seen it happen so often. Women tend to know better. They *want* to want to find out what people's concerns really are and meet them. They are not so ego-prone when they approach the bargaining table. That's how I passed the landmark model nursing-home law in Missouri. That's how I intend to work within the Caucus: avoiding confrontation, encouraging collegiality, listening, adjusting, adapting."

PEGGY: "That's a political artform women are perfecting. Toss out an idea, listen to feedback, invite debate, throw it in the pot, and stir until you reach consensus."

CATHERINE: "That strikes a chord. One of the things that was exciting to me while writing *Composing a Life* was looking at the way women deal with conflicting priorities, and with interruptions and transitions in their lives and learning to adapt, to keep all the balls in the air. Women who are successful in bridging discontinuities in their lives are women who are successful in finding ways in which their accomplishments continue to resonate. Then their learning carries over."

Needing a reality check on the dynamics between women and political parties, Catherine clarifies the relationship for us: "Access to political office is completely controlled in both parties. I think when we talk Republican and Democrat, we are buying a polarization that is not to our advantage. We should question these divisions we did not create and that may not be good expressions of the way we need to see the world. They're win/lose propositions for women."

HARRIETT: "Right. That's partly my job in leading a bipartisan organization where Republican women sometimes feel aggrieved as a minority. Frankly, they're often a feminist and progressive minority within their own party.

"We have to be sure we can hold onto our gains, to learn ways to institutionalize what we do. If we don't keep it going we lose everything our individual energy and initiative have created. We have to train others to follow us. We go in, we do the job, but if we don't build a structure, we stand to lose it all."

ILENE: "I think Bill Moyers calls it 'generational stewardship.'

He filmed an incredibly moving documentary relating the environment and spirituality. A Native American Indian woman said, 'Well, you probably don't understand this, but every time our tribal council makes a decision, we must look eight generations ahead.'"

BETTE: "One reason institutions go down the tube is that the head honchos don't train those coming up behind them. I wondered if you had given thought to training the future leaders of your coalition, getting the older women to look over their shoulder at who's coming along behind, giving them a 'leg up'?"

HARRIETT: "Yes, among the specific goals I thought about as I took office were two kinds of training. The first was to train trainers to spread out and do that nuts-and-bolts work we must do to get women appointed and elected, and secondly to train those who will have to carry on."

## OLDER WOMEN AS POLITICIANS

*"Women enter the political arena twenty years later than their male competitors...women who have political clout are usually in their mid-fifties to late sixties..."*

Before tackling the counseling of the next generation of political leaders, it seems a good moment to take stock, to assess the place of older women in the current political picture. The average female candidate first enters the political arena twenty years later than her male competitor. She is going to have to close that experience gap at a dead run. And she usually does. A woman who reaches a powerful political position in America is, statistically, over fifty. This defines both her handicap and her opportunity. In 1992, of the fifty-four women in the 103rd Congress, twenty-eight of them (more than half) had passed their fiftieth birthday: eleven were over fifty-five and eight over sixty. Three of the

country's four female governors are in the over-fifty-five category: Barbara Roberts (Oregon) is fifty-eight, Anne Richards
(Texas), sixty-one, and Joan Finney (Kansas), sixty-nine. Of
the four women appointed to Clinton's cabinet, three are
in their fifties; one is sixty-one. So, when we imagine
women who wield political clout, we are really looking at
women in their mid-fifties to late-sixties. By definition,
whether measuring numbers or drive, they dominate the
political picture.

To be positioned for a political race, most older women
have already learned to "layer." To catch up with the male
pack, they must be ready to do some serious risk-taking.
Both layering and risk-taking involve a new understanding
of the life cycle and what Catherine calls "second adulthood." Everyone wants to chip in on the concept that
women do, indeed, have a second chance to enter the
political arena. Harriett quickly correlates it to her own
experience.

HARRIETT: "When I was fifty I attended a conference on women
and power. I came away saying, 'It's too bad I'm too old to
run for the Senate.' Women in their forties assured me,
'You aren't,' and I thought, 'For a woman, that's too old.' I
was wrong. I had simply absorbed the mythology of what a
woman was capable of doing at different ages. Later I ran
twice for the Senate."

CATHERINE: "I think we can all remember saying, 'Oh, I'm too
old to do this,' and then doing just that years later."

HARRIETT: "For so long there was this sense of women being
held to a different age qualification for public life. 'Should
I get a facelift or shouldn't I?' Not because you want to be
beautiful but because you are aware that society is going to
look at you and categorize you strictly according to your appearance, and in a different sense from the way they categorize men."

GAIL brings us back to "passages" to link women's growing political role and our changing perceptions of the life cycle: "Men have always been able to start over, often several times. Many of them opt for public life on the second go-round. Most younger women have also started to improvise on the traditional life cycle. We now understand that the markers in our lives are not set in concrete. We know that age norms for major life events have become highly elastic."

PAT: "I liked the way Catherine phrased it this morning—that you can be old in one sphere and very young in another. That you're layered with many different ages, often all out of sync. That captured my imagination."

GAIL: "I agree. I was asked to analyze a national survey of 1,500 Americans between eighteen and sixty-five. I'm interviewing women right now in what I call their 'flaming fifties.' They have either the chance to strike sparks against the shell of their earlier years or to refuse to expand. Certainly, mid-life crises no longer peak at the age of forty; there is going to be a much longer passage into old age. There will be time to jump into politics, climb Mount Everest. I'm toying with the term 'maturesence' to describe it—it's simply a new layer."

DENISE: "I see in your resumes that you've all learned to change hats as you go along. I love to adapt, to change scale. I work on regional economics of a downtown area, but I also love going to the millimeter on the design of a chair. I've had many career changes, from being an architect to being an academic, from being an academic to designing college campuses, and doing all of this while being a mother. It's a crazy quilt."

PEGGY: "So if we see the life cycle in Catherine's terms, as a 'composition,' then moving from being a mother to running for the Senate as 'a mom in tennis shoes' as Pattie Murphy [U.S. Senator, Washington] did, will seem comfortable.

Women will still join political life late, but will do it not as tokens or loners but in the company of a large cadre of older women who've learned the art of composing their lives as they go along."

GAIL: "I have a secret dream that joins risk and politics. I wish we could trigger the movement here at Esalen. If we, as mothers and grandmothers of girls and young women who don't know what it's like to go backwards, were to step forward and do something seemingly outrageous we could accomplish miracles—link arms across generations and march for choice in front of the Supreme Court. What an irresistible image for the media—what a way to see that the spirit of the sixties is not lost. What a way to make visual our bonding as we defend our gains."

## WOMEN AND POWER:
## THE WORLD VIEW

*"In the United Nations, one view is that women must be depicted as vulnerable because if they are NOT seen as needing help, assistance will be cut off."*

Bette is eager to enlarge the scope of our conversation. As Director of the Women's Initiative, she works with older women's issues on an international scale. Bette feels the need to stretch the parameters of our dialogue to include the deep divisions within the United Nations about the way policy makers should portray older women.

BETTE: "There are some of us who are trying to bring the perspective of older women to debates at the United Nations. Clearly, two diametrically opposing views have surfaced, dividing the worldwide women's movement into two hostile camps. One is that all older women must be depicted as vulnerable, because if they are not seen as needing help, assistance will be cut off. Then there are those of us who say that we should look at older women from the point of view of productive aging and the contributions they make to their communities and to the world."

VIRGINIA: "And what countries take that perspective?"

BETTE: "Working with the Office for the Advancement of Women, it's been fascinating to see which countries have taken which side. Canada believes that in order to help older women they must be portrayed as vulnerable. That's their first priority. The French, on the other hand, adopt the productive-aging paradigm. That surprised me. China is looking at productive aging as the way to go, as is most of Africa."

MARILYN: "When you present women as victims and as vulnerable, at whatever age, you are devaluing them. It's seeing only the negative side. People are not going to want to identify with that model, particularly younger women. They're going to say, 'Well, these women are whining, and they deserve what they get.' It's important to feel outraged about rape, child abuse, incest, but if you leave it only at that stage it turns out to be a double negative. You're taking away from women their sense of control over their own destiny. That's a very bad thing. You get into the self-fulfilling prophecy realm. We have to have the kind of agency that allows us to 'take back the night,' to actively respond to victimization rather than let it define us."

BETTE: "Some of the problem lies with definitions. When is a woman old? That differs from country to country. What does 'productive' mean? It differs from culture to culture. Isn't the grandmother in Africa productive when she stays behind in the village and takes care of the children while the parents work in the cities?"

CATHERINE: "If you're babysitting for your grandchildren, you're definitely productive!"

GINNY: "I'm uncomfortable with the word 'productive.' It gives the impression that unpaid work—volunteering—doesn't count. I prefer the concept of 'participating,' meaning actively involved. It says it all."

BETTE: "You're right. I'm happier with the word 'participatory.' I'll take it back to the UN."

Bette seems satisfied. We've taken our discussion of older women in politics all the way from the grassroots to the United Nations; we've raised questions that beg for future dialogue. Perhaps the Year of the Woman will give us some answers.

### A YEAR LATER

*"The 'Year of the Woman' in politics has arrived; the men are saying, 'If only I were a woman, I'd be a shoo-in.'"*

As we gather in front of the fireplace, it's now the summer of 1992 and the national election is only four months away. This time we have all carried heavier political baggage down the winding road to Esalen. The difference is palpable; we all feel the heightened tension, the raised expectations, a stronger sense that, at last, this will be *our* year. This time we will become visible, we will be listened to, we will be viewed as heavyweights. Political dynamics have changed dramatically; the pace is accelerated. We view it as telling that a male congressman up for re-election recently told Pat Schroeder (U.S. Congresswoman, Colorado), "If only I were a woman, I'd be a shoo-in." Older women are campaigning hard on every level. Voters are responding, and the latest polls are proving it.

Television reception does not extend across the coastal range, and we want desparately to watch the Democratic Convention. At last, a husband volunteers to play courier with tapes of each day's drama, and after dinner we settle down for our political fix.

Most of us are just high-spirited amateurs, but two in our 1992 semi-circle are political party pros. They had both been on convention floors and know the ropes, from opposite sides of the ring. Mary Louise Smith, as the only woman chair of a political party in the country's history, was the first woman to organize and call to order a national convention. In 1976 it was her rich contralto dominating the floor as she stood behind the podium for five days in control of the Republican Convention. All eyes are on her now, noting her body language and her expressions as she reacts to the Democratic Convention.

She often roars with laughter that seems to bubble up straight from the gut; she's a good sport. Sitting beside her, often affectionately clutching her arm, sits Libby Cater, who has also spent many hours on convention floors—all of them Democratic. In the 1960s, she could be seen moving among delegations serving as a political aide and link to the White House. She thrived for years in the competitive Johnson White House, working with Lady Bird Johnson on educational and environmental programs.

Mary Louise and Libby play off each other as we start our political dialogue.

## STYLE VS. SUBSTANCE:
## A SECOND OPINION

*"We're now looking at decision-making imaged as a web; women's style is becoming acceptable..."*

Peggy tosses out an initial teaser. The assumption is that in 1992 the political pundits have hit the mark, that eight women will be elected to the Senate and approximately sixty to the House. If they are correct, a host of questions naturally follow. Will such a groundswell signal both a substantive and a stylistic shift in national politics? Will it mean new legislation on age discrimination, housing, pension vesting? Will it generate a ripple effect into local politics, even the corporate sector?

LIBBY: "It's a new chemistry. We've gotten over that first hump when women felt they had to outdo men. Now we're not looking at a hierarchy but at decision-making imaged as a web. Women's style is becoming acceptable. Bringing everyone along could be the name of the new game in Washington."

MARY LOUISE: "But numbers don't tell the whole story. Women don't all agree. To rely on numbers gives the wrong impression. It's true, we have our own style, but we still have to perfect the art of consensus building, of negotiating with men."

ELLIE: "Let's start by using new words. The two styles should really be termed 'alpha' and 'beta'—quick, decisive problem solving versus long-term cooperation and acceptance. Men have a vested interest in remaining dominant. If women's style proves effective, they will adopt it to stay on top. The bottom line is this: get in the system and get things done. If it takes adopting men's style, then do it. Sometimes I love aspects of men's management style. It's clean, you know 'Who's on first?' Style will follow results—both men and women will eventually learn the best of both techniques."

IRENE: "Let's not forget men have gone along. The Congressional Caucus on Women's Issues has more male members than female. Women's issues have passed on men's votes."

PAT: "All the recent exit polls show men often cross over on gender issues. I wonder if we are really capitalizing on this."

MARY LOUISE: "If we can show men it's good politics to go along with women's issues, we can trade votes to get what we want."

JUDY: "Now you have hit on the whole point. Bottom line: they don't vote on our issues, we don't vote for them."

MARY LOUISE: "We're not talking purity here."

ELLIE: "We have to learn the art of horsetrading. Pat Schroeder has described how she had to scramble and strategize to get on the Armed Services Committee."

PEGGY: "You're right. Politics isn't just about ideology. It's about getting things done, it's about process. And that isn't always pretty.

VIRGINIA: "As I remember, she had to call in all her 'due chips' from the men she had supported. Pat had to trust the political leverage she had accumulated over the years and bet everything on one key move."

ELLIE: "I believe in the concept of 'critical mass,' which was tested and found true in the civil-rights movement. You have to amass 33 percent of the political weight. Once you have done that, you can change the dominant culture. What we are witnessing this year doesn't do it. Even if we meet the predicted numbers, it's not enough of a shift. Also, we should remind ourselves that we aren't looking at reality on TV. It's a false perception. The media has given women a disproportionate visibility out of sync with their actual numbers."

PEGGY: "Is it fair to say women let themselves be co-opted into the men's establishment to give their agenda a fair shot? Harriett feels that women should maintain their style in the face of pressure, and even defeat, on issues. I seem to hear us saying here that it's more essential to win on the issues, to climb the power structure, than to remain stylistically pure. Have I got it right?"

ELLIE: "Yes. The heart of the matter is to win on the issues. Our first priority should be 'get in and move up.' This is particularly true for older women. An apt analogy: the swimmer crossing the river holding clothes above her head to keep them dry. She misses the point—the main thing is to reach the other bank. Cross the river and *then* worry about ideals. Men are not used to talking things through; they are action-oriented. To get our needs met, we need to learn to play by their rules, be one of 'the boys' if we have to. Questions of style are a luxury."

ILENE: "Well then, as older women, let's list some of the issues that are significant enough to warrant sacrificing a clear-cut feminist style and even a purist sense of idealism."

JUDY: "Age-discrimination laws need to be tightened. A producer for NBC fired a block of employees and hired new people under thirty-five. The older ones had to sign off on severance pay and pensions. We shouldn't stand for that."

LIBBY: "Health insurance with priority given to long-term care; after all, we are the caregivers."

IRENE: "Absolutely. We need to support the best coalitions we have on this. We need to help the Women's Health Network, which draws both media and public attention to women's health problems, to stay on track and focused."

PAT: "I see another problem that is seldom discussed. Husbands die or retire and older women are left with no access to health coverage. We are talking large numbers here. On an average there is a fifteen-year window of vulnerability, a gaping dark hole we have to close."

IRENE: "A lot of older women fall through that crack. You're talking about a very real issue, although new studies show that the situation is improving. But I have another complaint. Most breast cancer experiments were done on men, not on women. We need, at the very least, a level playing field in health research. If we really push, we can get line items on these."

GWEN: "We need more studies on osteoporosis and incontinence."

IRENE: "What we in this room really need to push for is a

Select Committee on Older Women, patterned after the late Congressman Claude Pepper's successful Committee on Aging. If we are going for policy reforms, let's give them staying power."

## WEAVING A WEB OF SUPPORT

*"Let's not reinvent the wheel...let's link up with it."*

We begin to evaluate the range and depth of the institutionalized help older women can count on. Even if all the women running in the upcoming election were to win, how strong and resilient is our supportive web in the current political climate? Change and hope are certainly in the air, but can we be certain the safety net is secure enough to withstand the political backlash which will inevitably follow change? The news is both reassuring and discouraging. Every study shows that women officeholders who are closely tied to women's organizations remain in office longer and go out further on a limb to reshape public policy. They are inclined to be risk-takers. But are organizations that target older women's issues ready to come to their rescue? It's not a sure bet. As a safety net, our patchwork of women's organizations obviously needs mending.

JANE: "NOW (National Organization for Woman) really does nothing to promote older women's issues. It needs to be pressed into an activist role. The impact of AARP on women's issues is so small one could put it into a thimble."

GWEN: "You have to give it credit. I've worked with the AARP Women's Division a lot and it does do well on health. If we are going to attack it, let's do it for the right reasons. Their record on minority issues and pension vesting for women is consistently strong."

PEGGY: "The Women's Division of the AARP did in fact produce an extensive study on older women and divorce. It's a dynamite package for older women who can't afford legal help."

IRENE: "Their strength is in their local offices and social clubs, and their advice on taxes and voting."

VIRGINIA: "Then when and why did the AARP shut down the Women's Initiative?"

PAT: "It happened quietly, about six months ago. It was placed under the wing of the Division of Handicapped and Minorities. For all intents and purposes, it lost its muscle. Ironically, it had the financial backing to make older women visible and the research potential to back up the courage and clout of other women's groups."

The talk continues, fragmentary and unfocused, drifting over the Grey Panthers and the White House Conferences on Aging, until OWL is mentioned. It alone strikes a chord; everyone is curious, leaning forward, wanting to know more.

GWEN: "The Older Women's League should be supported. They are truly effective—with a tremendous track record as lobbyists and tough legislative infighters."

JANE: "I like their strategy: 'Don't Agonize—Organize!' They are pragmatists, focusing in on just three issues every year. Their real strength is networking. With a base in Washington D.C., they bring together all like-minded groups inside 'The Beltway.' Their potential is enormous. They are professional coalition builders with an instinctive sense of outreach, of knowing where the 'hot buttons' are hidden."

GWEN: "They can't do as much as they'd like. They operate on a very small budget and with a relatively small and scattered membership."

ILENE: "Joan Kuriansky, their executive director, was slated to be with us, but her mother was seriously ill. She wanted to be kept aware of what happened here. We'll pass it all along."

GWEN: "This is the organization we should plug into. Tish Summers started it on the West Coast. Their core of support still comes from Northern California."

JANE: "OWL is a real grassroots movement that's given us a way to lobby and network. Let's not reinvent the wheel here — let's link up with it."

### BACK TO BASICS

*"Stamp-licking is no longer perceived as a way of moving up the political ladder."*

MARY LOUISE: "We're blinded by tunnel vision here. We have a tendency to look only at women at the top of the power pyramid. We should be looking at older women's participation back home. *They* are the ones who ultimately make women in politics happen. *They* are the ones who get out the vote and send women to state legislatures. We are doing miserably at the grassroots level. We could be immensely powerful if older women were active at the local level. We need to become involved in party organizations and sustain those already in office. We need to serve as foot soldiers again, to lick stamps, make the calls. Those fundamental enabling jobs are avoided. We need to build up the underpinning, to create a positive image of the political volunteer."

VIRGINIA: "Are you saying we jumped the gun by putting so much emphasis on the national level?"

MARY LOUISE: "I'm saying that it's still a man's world and you don't change it by just changing the top level. We have to be willing to be foot soldiers again, go back into the trenches, if we want to sustain what we have."

ELLIE: "Stamp-licking is no longer perceived as a way of moving up the political ladder."

IRENE: "We need power all the way up. We need the old sense

of cadre. Younger women don't have time to put on the
pressure—we have to turn out the cadres of older women
all along the line."

MARY LOUISE: "We need to reduce the fear factor. I think older
women who have made it to the top are perceived as a
threat. I believe I'm threatening to other women. Sometimes I feel I'm a nag about bringing older women into the
decision-making process. And I worry women are seen as
potentially potent only on the domestic front. For instance,
why are we ignoring the fact that older women have played
a significant role in peacemaking? If they're not in the field,
we ought to raise them up."

CLAIRE: "Someone recently said, 'The only way to save civiliza-
tion is for the men to use their feminine side and have
women help them.'"

SALLY: "When I started doing my work with peace organizations, there was only a grassroots involvement on the part of
women; very few women were being trained for high-level
responsibilities. It was certainly true at the United Nations.
Maybe it's because there aren't any warlike women."

MARY LOUISE: "It's a natural role for women to play. But even
at the State Department level, and in my own Institute, it's
an uphill battle. My question is, 'How long?' Do we just
keep up the pressure?"

JUDITH: "Older women need to speak out. A recent news story
proves it can work. In the midst of riots and looting in Rus-
sia, the older women of one community got together and
demanded that the revolution be brought under control.
The leaders stepped in and stopped the bloodshed."

MARY LOUISE: "I'm afraid the perception of strong women also
creates animosity toward them. When we 'do our thing,' on
the one hand we feel gratified at the results we can see, and
on the other we alienate people who say, 'There she goes
again.'"

SALLY: "Can we sit there silently? I can't. The difference is dramatic when women participate in politics. When older women get together, it's powerful. They can make change happen."

MARY LOUISE: "Yes, I have measured it."

ELLIE: "Then why have we remained invisible in the political arena? Studies say we have been made to feel invisible by male behavior, by men exerting unconscious hostility toward us. It's a good way of keeping women out of public conversation, a weapon in the 'war between the sexes.' If we venture into public life, we are perceived as poaching on their territory."

MARY LOUISE: "I have a problem relating to that. Obviously, I never was visible until I was sixty. Maybe it's because I come from the Midwest where things are much more realistically viewed. If I were to carry this message back with me—about really empowering older women—much of the conversation here would simply pass them by. This is not what they want to hear, it is not what they want to know. They want to know the practicalities of what happens after sixty. You're simply not reaching them on their level. If you talk of empowerment or political visibility, you'd lose them before you started. I don't mean to be critical; I will grow from this experience. I'm simply saying that to take this dialogue back to the women I talk to, I'd have to pick and choose."

LIBBY: "I don't think for a minute that this conversation would play well in Peoria. It would have to be distilled, given focus. It wouldn't work where women have consistently denigrated themselves, internalized negative images about what it means to be an older woman in this society. You are different, Mary Louise—you've had strong, proud, admirable women as role models and you just sailed ahead."

MARY LOUISE: "It may be like saying we don't know what it's like to be black because we've never been black."

LIBBY: "Exactly. You have to understand your audience. At the Aspen Institute, a think-tank that holds seminars on current social issues, the object is to get together opinion makers and let ideas fly free. They then pick and choose the information that will work in their arena."

A general sense of unease indicates there's something left unsaid. Judy and Mary Louise deal with it head on. It gives us all permission to feel insecure about taking the leap into public life: coming clean about our fear somehow makes us feel stronger.

JUDY: "The riskiest job is doing a politically sensitive documentary. I'm in the process of doing one on World War II with Walter Cronkite. A friend and colleague of mine put it well: 'I'm not afraid of dying; I'm afraid of failing publicly.' Any time you are creating, you are risking...you're perpetually insecure."

MARY LOUISE: "I think older women cannot be successful without risk-taking. I became head of the Republican party in 1974 and didn't think ahead to the fact that I would have to preside over the convention of 1976. Calling that convention to order was very scary—I was literally shaking. But I realized that, had I resigned, the convention would have turned the podium over to a male. I couldn't let that happen. So I got all the help I could and went forward. Doing nothing would have risked my whole career. My biggest disappointment was that, when Ford was in office, we didn't go ahead and ratify the ERA. My greatest risk right now is saying what I think, following my heart, and still remaining a Republican."

JUDY: "I love your guts!"

She spoke for all of us. Taking off for an afternoon hike through the redwoods, feeling high about older women, their values, talents, and sheer nerve, we jog down the trail, looking forward to what might lie around the next bend.

# CHAPTER SIX

# The Career Woman

We approach the dialogue about women in the public and professional sphere with a degree of smugness. It seems simple and predictable. We knew where *this* topic would take us: to problems of "the glass ceiling," "Leveling the Playing Field," "the old boys' network," and the prickly thickets of sexual harassment.

We're dead wrong. Our participants aren't buying that agenda. *They* want to head in new directions, to talk about questions of the optimum balance between professional and family life, the recycling of skills and accumulated wisdom, and to define the special decision-making style women bring to their professional lives. They want to share their early professional fantasies and their regrets at career paths not taken. And they're anxious to see how their experience might help realize their daughters'—and granddaughters'—dreams.

## DIFFICULT CHOICES, MULTIPLE ROLES

*"We're doing what's necessary...slugging it out now so the next generation might have more equality in relationships between men and women...."*

Over the past three decades, many women have faced an

increasing tension between the pull of family ties and the push of personal ambition. There are tough trade-offs involved.

LIBBY: "I think it's a terribly exciting time for women in public life...the fact that they *do* approach problems differently. Women are tired of the way things have been done: it's fresh — it's *really* a change!"

JANE: "That's a good point, and it defines something about the New Older Woman: she renegotiates her relationships every day — with her husband, her kids, her parents, her friends, and her colleagues. She renegotiates her relationships because she's a different person now, and it's required if she's going to maintain her new status."

JUDITH: "Many older women think equality is something you say the *next* generation will do better at. But I say *no!* It's the *women* who are slugging it out now, in marriages, in relationships, in careers, and they're doing what's necessary so that the *next* generation might have more equality in relationships between men and women."

LIBBY: "I have two daughters, and they are the ones who would say, 'Mom, why are *we* always clearing up the dishes and making the beds when those two big beautiful lugs (their brothers) are just taking out the garbage and mowing the lawn? It isn't right!' And about that same time, Judith Moyers wrote asking me, 'What are you doing, where are you fitting in, what do you think of all this new writing?' Well, I hadn't even looked at it. She listed the books she was reading, and one of them was Betty Friedan's book, *The Feminine Mystique*. I got it, and the scales fell from my eyes, and I said, 'Whoa!' It was just a real awakening.

"I think my daughters were the first ones that said, 'We're not going to put up with this!' And they were very excited when I got involved in the Aspen Institute, and we had workshops about the changing roles of women. Now, I watch them and my heart almost breaks. My youngest daughter, who is in film-making and has two small children, says, 'Mom, for my self-esteem I feel I just *have* to try to keep up my film-making, but these two kids are my heart and my life. The biggest issue for us (her husband is a San Francisco publisher) is that we fight about who's going to get up at 4:30 a.m. to feed the baby!' This is because she has to be at work and in touch with the East Coast early, and he needs to be working by 5 a.m., so they argue about who will have the privilege of that time with the baby. They can't both do it, or they'd be wiped out by the end of the day. So here are two people fighting to take this small space of time at 4:30 in the morning. My daughters helped pull me up — and I've learned so much from them.

"The big problem for me is breaking the pattern that I learned from my own mother, of compulsively doing really *nice* things for others. She did it to the extent that she was considered a martyr. And I have to break this habit of self-denial — when you deny yourself this so you can accomplish that. That kind of self-denial is so ingrained in me that now, when I have a chance for some time, I find myself still doing those things I've been doing for years. I want to break this habit and I want to get away from being so goal-oriented. Each day I have these lists, like we all do, but I'll never be on top of it all. I've got to accept that. But now, with a room and a computer, at the top of the list is, 'Two hours of creativity each morning!' — and do it *first!*"

The group responds with empathy and shared frustration. Libby continues: "Now my life's at a critical stage where I'm going to carve out a *new* life. I'm hoping to get my husband out of my workspace; he takes over every room I've ever set up. He encouraged me to come here, but I remember he said, 'Will you still be speaking to me when you get back?' He's a guy with an open mind, but he also wants to be in control. So, when I got this room all set up with files and drawers and the door closed, he said 'What are you *doing* up there?'" A chorus of understanding groans greets Libby's story.

VIRGINIA: "We could spend a day just on the implications of 'a room of one's own.'"

LIBBY: "My daughters were so concerned for me when they knew I was coming here because, although I had always been involved politically, I never plugged all the way in. I mean I didn't have the credentials or the tenure, like Irene or other women in this room who have Ph.D.'s. But my daughters said, 'Mother, you've had a *great* life-experience; don't feel put down. Just tell them about the time you had lunch with Nehru!"

JANE: "Actually, our daughters *need* us to be strong!"

JUDY relates that she followed a different path: "I got into my career accidentally. My own life has been different from women who are even ten years younger than I am. I got into a career simply because I wasn't married, but I did not have a grandiose career plan about where I would be five years from now, ten years from then. I just sort of did the best job that I could wherever I was. I assumed that whatever would be, would be, and I don't know whether that's right or wrong, but it might be typical of my age group. I couldn't believe they'd *pay* anybody to go around learning what I had to learn! My business has changed in many ways, and commercial TV has, to a large extent, abandoned my field, which is documentaries."

ELLIE: "Sometimes women back off from their careers because they feel their success might hurt their man. They *worry* for him, as if a man without his pride is like a penis without an erection! It seems to me, what men need to learn is that they don't *have* to prove they're superior, or to dominate someone. The same applies to each sex; there are no more superior men than superior women. It's a delicate balancing act. Men can understand the desire to have an affair, but the idea of a woman seeking any form of autonomy is not part of their vocabulary. I've been working on this for some time, and I've come up with something I call 'Pot Roast Therapy.' If I move ahead too quickly in being a feminist, I cook my man a pot roast and it reassures him. It's a tangible symbol of security. I'm not abandoning my commitment to family. I slow down for a while, I pace my career moves."

SALLY: "Men's ego status comes from their work; our total ego does *not* come only from our profession."

LIBBY concurs: "The majority of men we know who have retired were in powerful professional positions; their identities were connected to their work. So now they're going mad trying to fill that void."

Several voices compete to be heard; they're eager to express approval of the steps men of all ages are taking to become sensitive to the needs of their partners. There is agreement that as men understand their own roles in relationships, they become more supportive of women's needs to strike out on career courses.

JANE: "Thank God for Robert Bly and people like him who are saying to men, 'Look, you need to be there for each other, in whatever way that means to you.'"

DENISE: "I, too, feel that the women's movement has been great for men. Great for women, but also great for men. It's given men the opportunity to acknowledge their nurturing side, to be able to be loving fathers, which is wonderful for them and also for the kids. The men's movement, which started out with care and nurturing, is now thinking about what it means to be a warrior. The cross-fertilization will come there too; some people will discover that there are women warriors, too."

PEGGY: "As men age, they *do* seem to become gentler. My husband belongs to a Robert Bly consciousness-raising group. I've observed incredible changes in his attitude toward both men and women. He's certainly more supportive of my career goals; he cooks and cleans when I'm under pressure. What I've seen is evidence that there *are* older men who have demonstrated that they are ready to learn, to become more sensitive. When I see women discouraging and disparaging this kind of interaction between men, I think they're actually being self-destructive."

IRENE: "The Robert Bly movement is an acknowledgement of the male's realization that there are many good things in the female psyche that men should allow themselves to feel comfortable about emulating."

PEGGY speaks softly, from personal and painful experience: "Yes, that has been brought home to me since my husband, Chuck, became ill. I had the unique experience of listening in on his group one night. I was amazed, and deeply moved, by what I heard coming up the furnace-pipes from our garage downstairs, where they met. The drumming came first: powerful, masculine. Then the quiet Native American healing chants, as they massaged Chuck's body. And finally, the soft humming as nine pairs of hands lifted my husband's cancer-riddled body into the air for perhaps fifteen minutes: they were passing into him their collective energy. When it was all over, he climbed the stairs, and told me he felt revitalized. On those nights he could sleep—and so could I."

There was a long silence. Then Jane said, quietly: "The New Older Man isn't here yet—but perhaps we can hear him approaching."

## PERSONAL VS. PROFESSIONAL PRIORTIES

*"The notion that you can do it all...that's hard enough in your thirties..."*

Forging ahead in the public arena is a delicate balancing act between a woman's professional and personal priorities.

Peggy, attending a Vassar College reunion, asked the Class of '52 what the top priority was for their sixth decade. They answered that they wanted to achieve an equilibrium, hopefully comfortable and potentially rewarding, between the personal and the public aspects of their lives.

At Esalen, the consensus is that we must stay on course, even as we face hazards to our personal momentum: age discrimination, financial dependence, and negative stereotyping. The most painful and, potentially, the most crippling obstacle to attaining professional achievement, is the need for family caregiving, a reality for most families by the time women reach their mid-fifties.

HARRIETT puts the dilemma squarely: "How do we balance the instinct to care for others, and the *need* to care for others, against the limits it may place on your own life, and the guilt—in some cases the pain—that may come with it?"

SYLVIA EARLE, who has balanced her multiple roles as inventor, deep-sea explorer, chief of a governmental agency, and head of her own business with being mother, grandmother, and caretaker of her own ninety-four-year-old mother, responds with characteristic discipline: "One simply goes ahead—head up and shoulders back."

CATHERINE: "I worry about people being simultaneously blindsided and trapped by the caregiving...as when you are sixty-five and caring for your mother. People say to me, 'I'm retiring so that I can look after my mother'. That's a totally different juxtaposition and something that can block that new opening that goes with the end of the reproductive years. Similarly, there is the decline and dying of husbands—we *really* have to talk about the problems associated wth the demands of caring for a husband. I think of a friend of mine who really just came into her own professionally when her husband became dependent and infirm. He really wanted her to be 'Mama' and to abandon this blooming that she was experiencing. But she simply didn't have the energies to meet his demands. The notion that you can do it all, that you can care for children and be professionally active in a career, that's hard enough in your thirties! But the notion that you can start a brand-new chapter of your professional career in your sixties or seventies *and* care for someone who is becoming increasingly dependent, is a very difficult one."

HARRIETT: "By this age, we're much more sensitive to the need for caregiving, and I like all that is being said. At the same time, we have to be aware that it may be oppressive if we don't deal with it in the proper way. We talk about the kids coming home: that could be an enrichment, but it can also be an oppression. And now we talk about taking care of our aging parents: it can also bring a lot of guilt and oppression. I think many of us are experiencing that...and it can be limiting."

She poses another dilemma: "Many of our husbands are older than we are. And we have to ask ourselves, 'Can I go on fulfilling my responsibilities as a caregiver...what is my choice?' I don't know but I think I must struggle with it."

We concede there are no easy answers and agree that personal strengths or weaknesses will be tapped in weighing caregiving decisions against career satisfactions. Harriett is right: formulating such choices is a struggle.

Catherine suggests another barrier women face as they choose a career. This time the catch-22 centers on age discrimination, especially in academia.

CATHERINE: "Another part of the picture is somebody who goes back to school in what should now be a different climate. They go back at forty-five and get a Ph.D. and finish it, *then* they're discriminated against on the grounds of age. You can't say I'm a *new* Ph.D."

GAIL: "Does tenure cut off at a certain age everywhere? Is it forty, or fifty? I mean, you can't start gaining points toward tenure after a certain age. Is that right?"

PEGGY: "No, that would be age discrimination. But indeed, it's still there. After all, they don't want to start paying a pension in only seven or eight years...there are lots of issues. I got my Ph.D. at fifty-three, and I've had a tough time. For me, the tenure track is pretty much, quietly, closed."

CATHERINE: "But it's the same thing in law firms. The point is, there's an unstated age by which you're supposed to have *made* it. And if you haven't made it by that age, you're a permanent outsider; you're out of step."

PAT: "So it's a discouraging thing for the older woman. She goes back and retools, or goes around for the first time—having dealt with raising children and caring for a husband and his career, then finds that she's over the hill."

MARILYN: "It certainly is true that a person who is female— well, should have an advantage these days: *should* have. And if you are an ethnic minority, you should have an advantage. But nothing has been done in favor of older people, and particularly older women. That subject is taboo. I think that the advantages that some women are experiencing in the educational world, particularly in higher education and in the job market, just haven't been translated into the age groups where women need it the most. The older you are, the less you get, and after a certain point, you don't get anything. I think to some extent it's true in the business world as well."

BETTE: "That's true, too. Companies don't often promote older women, even if the older woman is a star, because she's 'too old' and 'won't be around long enough.' They don't invest when there's not enough return..."

MARILYN: "Many women *do* have to slow down the pace of their work during the childbearing years; but after forty, forty-five, fifty—this is when most women are released from those responsibilities. And these should, in fact, be the most productive years for women. That's where the prejudice against older people, and older women in particular, is the most insidious. And I think that this is really something we haven't confronted in the same way that affirmative-action programs have confronted the gender and the minority issue. It's still untouched territory."

PEGGY: "Ironically, businesses question your sense of commitment as you come into the labor market at fifty: 'What were you doing at thirty? What were you doing at thirty-five?' You are suddenly not authentic. And I think this is sad, because you may be *very* authentic, *very* committed."

### PRIDE, PREJUDICE AND PARTNERSHIP: ONE WOMAN'S CAREER PATH

*"One theme in my life is sexism and the star-system in architecture."*

Suffering from travel fatigue and a back problem, Denise eschews the floor pillows-and-sweatsuits mode the rest of us choose. She requests and gets a proper chair, accepts a cup of tea, and launches into the saga of her life as a public woman and partner in the architectural firm Venturi, Scott Brown & Associates, Inc. of Philadelphia. The firm has been responsible for some of the world's most publicized and innovative structures; in fact, Denise and her husband, Robert Venturi, have just returned from the dedication of the new wing of the National Gallery in London, which they designed. If not exactly typical of all women's career problems, hers has much in common with many women's workplace tales.

DENISE: "One theme in my life is sexism and the star-system in architecture. I wrote an article about it called *Room at the Top: Sexism and the Star System in Architecture*. It caused such anger toward our firm from others in the field that I didn't publish it until 1989. (Emily Handcock, Faucett, 1990). Now I get all kinds of comments from women in all fields about it, although I don't think most architects have read it yet. At the last ACSA (Association of Collegiate Schools of Architecture) conference I went to, someone mentioned the Pritzker Prize for Architecture, a prestigious professional award presented to Robert Venturi in 1991, and before I could answer, someone else asked, 'Why didn't it go to *you*, too?' And that group of architectural educators, both women *and* men, were outraged. Five years ago, only the women would have felt the slight. So, I think it's improving.

"Bob and I were faculty colleagues at the University of Pennsylvania; when we married, there were three of us — partners in this struggling little firm. Or, rather, I was not a partner until 1969. My name was not added to the firm until 1980, owing to my partners' worries about changing the firm's identity. As soon as Bob and I married, I was looked upon as the typist and photographer for my husband by the architectural media and the profession, and I've fought that ever since. Even now, people will say to me, 'We were wondering what you do in the firm, Denise. We gather you're the accountant.' That was in England, just last week!

"And although one says that our firm got the Pritzker Prize, our *firm* did not get the Pritzker Prize; Robert Venturi got the Pritzker. There was bitter acrimony, they tell me, in the jury, as some of the people who knew us tried to say it should be given to both of us. But the critics writing about great art in architecture try to make their way by crowning a king. And you can't crown a mom and pop king. There are no female prima donnas in architecture!

"I am now running many aspects of the firm, managing in many more varied ways than before, while still carrying on my design work and running my planning projects, and—Lord save me!—trying to bring in work. And suddenly everyone is looking to me and smiling. I feel I've had a new blooming. At the moment, despite my attribution fights, I'm loving the projects I'm working on.

"I've meshed together my work, my child-raising, my home. We had our child by adoption, late in our lives, so we could afford a housekeeper. If we hadn't, I would have been out of architecture long ago. I try to juggle all the demands made on my time and energy. As it is, someone described our office as 'a high-wire act over Niagara Falls.'

"I'm very interested in our office as a place where men and women work together. Sometimes I have to admonish the women, 'That's not appropriate behavior, and it's no good accusing the male staff members of sexism. They just didn't want you to do this or that; I don't believe it was sexism.' And I say to the men, 'Look, I'm going to do this whether you like it or not, and I'm the boss, and there it is. Do the best you can.' But, I'm *not* going to let them put me down. So it's interesting. I find I can be a business person, which I didn't think I'd be, and I find I can talk heart-to-heart with people and get them to listen. And that brings a sense of power, too.

"For a long time, I used to say that I preferred the company of men. I liked what men talked about more than what women talk about. Then I discovered there were other women like myself who preferred the company of men, and I liked *them* as well as men. Those women and I were the ones who joined the women's movement. I still kept my scorn for women who were typists and homemakers. At one point during this stage of my emancipation, I wrote an angry letter to the press when my authorship was not attributed in reference to an article I wrote in collaboration with Robert Venturi. 'Do you think I'm my husband's typist?' But the typist put in a footnote: 'No, *I* am!' And I thought, 'I can't do that to her. If we don't all go up together, then none of us will.' Now, I realize that women and men have to reassign, and more broadly share, roles and respect, and I now enjoy the company of all types of women. I like talking with women who are full-time homemakers. They're *really* the executives. I attended a conference of the International Union of Women in Architecture, (headquarters, Paris), in Iran in 1976. A few of us were older than the others. The younger women trusted me. They wanted to talk about what it was like to have a baby. It was very moving: they couldn't ask their mothers. I said, 'You can't imagine anything more wonderful than having the baby sitting right there on the drawing board!'

"So, I say that architecture is my window on the world. And I see my role in management as finding a suitable structure for our firm, one that helps us artists operate a well-run business, yet achieves maximum creativity for all our members—even though it's very difficult to delegate in the arts. I try to identify problems, move in to solve them, get things worked out, then get myself the hell out and on to the next problem."

## INVENTING STYLES, RECYCLING SKILLS

*"I've had a patchwork background...nearly fifty careers!"*

Everyone agrees that developing a more feminine decision-making style, one that reflects a woman's natural talents for consensus-building, can be used as a point of departure for the leap through the glass ceiling. Recycling and reinventing skills that served her well as homemaker and a volunteer is another.

We start with basics. Women who attended college can still hear their professors say, "Define your terms first!" And so, like students, we frame the question: "*Is* there a feminine decision-making style that is clearly distinct from the masculine mode?" Surprisingly, consensus comes easily. Heads nodding, we agree that the difference is significant. PEGGY describes it this way: male decision-makers tend to think in tight, patterned, hierarchical terms. Envision a pyramid: access is strictly limited, debate is controlled, and usually dictated by a psychological phenomenon that political analyst Irving Janus calls "Group Think," in which the strongest male in the room dominates. Outcomes contain few surprises. Open communications, honest controversy, and a range of choices are traded for efficiency and decisiveness.

"The female style tends to be looser, more flexible. Envision a wheel, the spokes feeding inward to the hub. Access is open, debate is encouraged, participants play off each other. Everyone involved is expected to be seated around the bargaining table, talking frankly, listening carefully, testing options. Tradeoffs are more subtle: it takes more time, triggers more stress, and uses up more energy and skill in setting priorities. But these are rewarded by moments of true creativity, unexpected leaps over old barriers, and a sense of loyal and responsive teamwork."

CATHERINE: "The fact is, it's the norm now for people to be able to be and want to be productive for several decades longer than was the norm in the past. The question, then, arises: are we going to be just like the men, or does the difference reflect reality? Are we going to have to look at a whole generation, not just remaining active, not just continuing to work or deferring retirement, but continuing to develop new modalities and styles? The analogy that I have in my mind is the difference between working as a woman in a society where only a tiny fraction of women have careers."

PEGGY picks up on the analogy: "And that fraction hit a glass ceiling just as they hit their stride, usually in their fifties. They're effectively stymied by a structured, cohesive old-boys' ladder. The stats say it all. According to *Forbes* magazine, 'out of eight hundred CEOs, only two are women.' *Business Week* claims that of all the top women CEOs surveyed, only three are over fifty."

DENISE: "Those stats speak for me. There's a very tough glass ceiling in architecture. About ten years into the profession, women realize they're not getting to be project managers the way the men are. If they don't have some kind of feminist awareness, they're going to think it's their fault. They'll be effectively stopped in their tracks."

PEGGY: "The public woman has to be aware that failure is structured into her career ladder."

CLAIRE: "Yes, we have to learn to accept failure; to accept failure is a big, big asset! We learn the *fear* of failure—learning only begins *after* you fail."

ILENE: "Does 'women's intuition' play a role in this?"

RUTH B.: "Even in the corporate world, I think sudden, intuitive impulses have value. You find that because you made a certain phone call, all kinds of things fall into place."

GAIL: "I think intuition is one of the things that we tend to train out of ourselves, or layer over as we try to adopt male problem-solving strategies."

Another key element in the New Older Woman's success is her ability to combine the skills she has developed throughout her adult life—learning, teaching, practicing her profession—along with mothering, mentoring, volunteering, and caretaking. In addition to recycling her skills, she must be open to new ideas and be ready to take certain risks in order to re-invent herself in a new career or context.

SYLVIA: "I hear variations on the theme, 'The older you get, the more you know'. Each life seems to represent building on the experiences that form the unique structure that each of us turns out to be. And maybe the loss of some things, whether it's mobility or a spouse, forces you to focus. Otherwise, you'd just be gathering all this information. You have to sit down and take stock and pull together all your life experiences and make something of them. Or else you'd just be racing around, gathering more and more, and never really pulling it all together and making something of it."

We turned to Bette as the case study of a person whose resume resembles a collage of recycled skills and information.

BETTE: "I describe my life as one in which I have backed into everything I've ever done. My first husband was French, and I married him after spending five years in Berlin as head of a translating unit. I graduated with degrees in Russian studies and Slavic languages, and went to the State Department as a foreign-service officer. They needed me desperately because I knew Russian, Polish, and old church Slavonic. By 1951, I was twenty-four and living in Germany, as our State Department representative in Berlin. After that, I made several career changes and got into computers. I taught marketing at the Wharton School of Economics at a time when they weren't even accepting female students. And then I became a lobbyist, first in California, then in Washington, D.C. A few years ago, I became director of AARP's Women's Initiative, which identifies, studies, and speaks to older women's issues throughout the social fabric of the United States as well as foreign cultures. So, I've had a patchwork background, and it's been fun. People have taken a lot of chances on me and my ability to recycle my skills."

CLAIRE: "You are a wonderful example of consolidating memory and imagination, re-inventing forms, and adapting them to different uses."

CATHERINE: "One of the things I did a little while ago was try to imagine if I hadn't been interrupted in each of my previous careers, what I might have ended up doing. What if

I had not gone to the Philippines with my husband...or hadn't responded to the job offer teaching Arabic literature and linguistics? If I had not had to leave Amherst College, might I still be Dean of Faculty? When I look at them, I see how much less I would have learned had I been allowed to follow my original road. The mode in which I live now is improvisational—inventing new ways to use my talent and experience, transfering what I've learned, and putting it together differently at each stage. And I'm probably going to have to do that at least once or twice more in the remaining years of my life cycle. So eventually, I'll find out what I'm going to be when I 'grow up.' "

HARRIETT: "There's one other thing, building on what Catherine is saying, and that is how a continual learning process of skill-building happens. And I think this is essential when you talk about caregiving and building institutions. Very often, in order to do that, you have to acquire *new* skills. I've noticed, even among our group, that we're all still trying to get information."

GAIL: "I liked Catherine's notion of the different ages in different aspects, different layers, of your life. I've always said that we have to continue to be willing to be amateurs. And that's what being willing to learn something new is. It is the willingness to say that, in one area of your life: 'I am now going to be a learner, a beginner, an amateur.' 'Amateur' literally means, one who loves. So that's what we were saying: to follow your love, to create new loves."

ELLIE isolated for us an area in which many older women have failed to apply or recycle old skills: mastering the computer. "We have to learn technologies that have been traditionally male dominated—like the computer. What a tool that is to communicate! Many of us who grew up in the fifties had anxiety about math and physics; now, it's computers. We have access to this great tool and should use its power.

We are *not* helpless old women: we are relevant, and should
not be intimidated by what's been labeled MALE."

CLAIRE the most senior participant, winds up the discussion
with a zinger: "Computers? I'm against them! I'm manual.
But, when I'm a little older, I might use one."


### FINANCIAL INDEPENDENCE

*"You respect yourself in earning money....it says you
value yourself."*

For the career woman, financial independence is the key to
building self-confidence. We talk of how we generate the
confidence to enter the public arena and further, how to
manage independent earnings and finances to sustain one's
momentum. We look at history, at the roller coaster ride
women have historically taken in moving toward a sense of
financial independence since the early 1940s.

Our mothers expected their husbands to do the planning. Many didn't even ask about financial matters; some
never learned to write a check, much less have their own
bank accounts. World War II changed all that. Women had
to take over the financial planning while their husbands
were gone. They went to work in war industries to supply
the huge labor force needed to keep the country going.
Many experienced the satisfaction of their own paychecks
and were never quite the same again. Yet current studies
show that many women still figure they don't need to do
any planning because "their husbands are taking care of
that."

Most older women still don't know how to balance a
check-book until it's a question of survival. Often, the impetus for creating fiscal responsibility is the result of an
emotional shock, such as a career crisis, illness, widowhood, or a broken marriage.

PEGGY: "Divorce sent me into a deep depression, but now I thank God for that jolt. It galvanized me into action. I had to do something if I wanted to survive. Sometimes you gather strength at critical times."

JANE: "When I first began to earn money I said, 'I'm going to control that money.' My man was very shocked, and I don't think he ever quite forgave me for that. He still thinks it's a very big issue. But that money is very empowering to me and very important; even a little bit of money."

ELLIE: "Now that I've gotten older and the children are gone, I decided to get control of half the money. Not because I wanted to use it, but because I wanted the decision-making power that goes with it. My husband was tremendously threatened by this. But I persisted. By dint of nagging, everything now is split down the middle; one half of it is mine. 'You're mortifying me: I won't be able to hold my head up,' he told me. Well, I went to the woman who was the head of the investment department of the brokerage firm, and I said, 'I'm going through my feminist period.' And she said, 'Good for you!' So, sometimes he grumbles, but I let him grumble. 'Better to have money and be unhappy,' as my mother would say. 'If you have the money, you can call a lot more shots; you can be *very* happy!'

"Now I can make decisions I could never make before about what that money is doing—whether it's resting, working, playing, or whatever. His idea is that money should work, work, work. 'Are you losing money?', he asks. 'No, the money is resting.' 'You're losing buying power!' he insists. I say: 'The money's still there.' I find that having money and my own office are both very empowering. My office has a sign that reads: 'IF THERE'S A FIRE, YOU MAY KNOCK.'"

JANE: "I find it difficult to set a fee for such things as speaking engagements; when I'm supportive of a group or a cause and I set a low fee, I'm not even met at the door. But when I get $3,000, I'm treated like a queen!"

ELLIE: "You respect yourself in earning money. A high fee says that you value yourself: 'I'm good and I'm worth it!' But it's hard to go against our training. No monetary value is placed on rearing children, managing those parties for thirty-two business associates, keeping the home. It angers women that they're doing jobs that don't get recognition— there's no status attached to it. How dare men say, 'It's not *your* money?'"

CLAIRE: "Health, wits, time—they make the triangle. Maybe put money in the center; if you don't have it, you'll be sleeping in the streets! Money buys time, services, machines, if you have the wits to put it all together."

## ADOLESCENT DREAMS, WOMEN'S REALITIES

*"Had I been mature enough at age twelve to look ahead, there is no way I could have dreamed all I've done..."*

Are we all satisfied with our life choices? Some of us feel a lingering sense of things left unsaid or unexplained, a desire to go back, perhaps to retrace our steps. At ten or eleven, you're certainly not looking or thinking about a sense of self. You just *are*. With adolescence we become self-conscious and lose that quality, that sense of self.

What were our dreams—what had we wanted to become? Were we in a profession that fulfilled our fantasies? Were there regrets for paths not taken, opportunities passed by? Or, had we perhaps become *more* than we could have imagined fifty or sixty years ago?

ELLIE led off: "I would not have taken off time from my profession when I had children; I blithely assumed I could go back. I lost a lot of power in my relationships. But I believe

I would have been stronger for my children and would have had more clout with my spouse if I had continued to work. I wouldn't do that again. I love psychology, and the children did not really need all that attention."

LIBBY: "I wanted to go to law school at Stanford, but I simply didn't have the nerve. If I could do it over, I'd go for it. I'd have liked to run for Congress, but I had strong reservations. It didn't seem worth it for a two-year term; one is always running. It's absurd to be always thinking of votes, and not issues, and there's too much pressure."

SALLY: "I do have one enormous regret: not to have studied one thing and become an expert in one field—I don't care what field, just to know it all. I missed that and just flew by the seat of my pants. I *do* know how to start up organizations and keep them going. I'm a professional starter. After college I did join a sculpture class taught by Bob Howard, and had some success in San Francisco. Now I live on quicksand."

IRENE: "I seem to be the only one here who went straight for my Ph.D., and I'd do the same again. I need to continually update my training in economics and political science for teaching women's studies and city planning because things are changing so fast. The issues are changing fast too, and I need to be able to adjust."

GWEN: "I would not have married at twenty and had kids at twenty-two; I would have gone on for a graduate degree. At my age it would have been a lot easier if I had had a powerful academic appointment rather than a tenuous one."

JANE: "Had I been mature enough at age twelve to look ahead, there is no way I could have dreamed all I've done; I'd have been amazed. I had the wonderful opportunity to raise seven kids. Judy and I were talking about the 'miraculous accident' that we can continue to write, publish, produce for television, and do all these fulfilling and exiting things during this second phase of life. I love it! If I could change anything, I would have liked to have had some entrepreneurship in my life—take ideas I've had and make them more useful to more people. Looking back on the years from fifty to almost seventy, I can say, 'I wouldn't have dreamed I could do what I've done.'"

JUDITH: "I agree with Jane. I had a nervous breakdown in my twenties, and had to fight for my life to pull out, but it gave me strength. I too would like to be an expert, master one real skill."

MARY LOUISE: "I wouldn't change anything. I've been happy with my life all along. At twelve, I had the sense of wanting to be something. How many people started out as a precinct worker and ended up as chair of a national party? Who would have dreamed it? I have one small regret: I should have studied harder in college. But marriage and graduate school were more of an either/or proposition in my time and I would have had to miss a part of my marriage. Otherwise, I'm happy."

ILENE: "Much as I enjoyed rearing three sons, did they really need me all that time? I wanted a career, but with my husband in law school, I deferred it; I substituted with a lot of volunteer work as our boys were growing up. I was off to conferences and began to be involved. I identify with what Sally said—just do it! And I also wish that I'd become an expert in one field; I know a lot of miscellaneous stuff. And like Jane, I would like to have carved out some sort of career with a wider scope; I love exposure to new ideas, people and places, and I regret not being able to speak any foreign languages well—that skill opens so many doors."

JUDY: "I identify with parts of this discussion. It would never have occurred to me at twelve that I would have the opportunity to produce award-winning documentaries. I wouldn't change my life; I *would* change commercial TV, but that's beyond anything I can affect. And I would like to have met my husband sooner."

PEGGY: "I started out on the right track, and just got lost. I gave the valedictory address at Carmel High, class of 1948, on 'Women in Politics.' It was met with almost complete silence. I was supposed to be talking about team spirit, cheerleaders, the football team. After college graduation, I married at twenty-three and had a child. After a divorce, I got a job teaching political science and was a fairly successful single parent for five years. Then I met and married a very supportive man who encouraged me to go to graduate school. I got a Ph.D. at fifty-three, did post-doc studies at fifty-four, and have been teaching ever since. I love the classroom, and I'm back on track—teaching 'Women in Politics.'"

VIRGINIA: "As a kid, I wanted to be a boy: they had better toys and more freedom and fun. In junior high and high school, girls had to take 'domestic arts' and learn to be good little homemakers, but boys got to take shop and make things and *do* things. Then I wanted to be a journalist (my ideal was 'Brenda Starr, Girl Reporter'). And when I was sixteen, I got a job as a copyboy (literally)—I was eager to be the first to leap to the call for 'Booooy!'—then graduated to reporter. I continued to do some writing and editing after I graduated from college, married, and moved to the Monterey Peninsula. Until this project came along, I felt I'd strayed from my path: it's revved me up again. It's the first time I've worked with other women, or interfaced with other women as a group, and I like it. So fullness comes, late in the season."

HARRIETT: "I was going to be a newspaper reporter, but I was not going to be on the society page; I was going to be in the news area. The editor of the *Herald American* called me in.

There was only one woman working there, and she was what was called the 'sob sister.' There was still somebody who ran around saying, 'Scoop, scoop, I've got a scoop!' It was a marvelous experience for me. And I'm still struggling with a lot of issues of not just gender, but what I can do with the rest of my life."

DENISE: "Aren't we all really saying here that there are a million different ways to be a woman...and a million different ways to balance your act?"

# CHAPTER SEVEN

# Getting Ready for the Bonus Years

The difference between the present-day woman and her counterpart of one hundred years ago is her need to plan for the much longer life she will live. She will require information in order to make her own choices—without the help of a husband or family male elder—the choices that will shape and determine the quality of her life in the bonus years ahead.

GINNY: "The years ahead hold a lot of fears for older women. Surveys conducted by the Institute on Human Aging where I work show that financial security and health are the two major issues they are concerned about when considering plans for their later years. I worked on a project at the University of California at Los Angeles which looked at pre-retirement planning models for changing people's attitudes, behaviors and information. Financial issues kept surfacing as the reason why people were willing to think about the future at all. They were also thinking about health, and finances entered into that as well. When older people are asked what they would do differently if they had to plan their future again, the number-one answer is 'I would have started planning much earlier.' Their hindsights are very good clues for us. Planning is a major issue."

## CREATING THE SAFETY NETS

*"Wouldn't you feel better about jumping into something
new if you knew a safety net was there?"*

BETTE: "Sometimes when there is order in your life, you are
better able to enjoy the present because you've taken care
of those things that are no longer hanging over your head.
More women are going to have to get pensions—many
women don't have them and that's part of the problem."

GINNY: "For most women, Social Security is either very low or
non-existent unless they're getting something from their
husband's Social Security."

DENISE: "You need to have problem-solving skills so you can
deal with contingencies."

CECELIA: "And some sense of confidence in one's self, in one's
decision-making capability."

BETTE: "You have to be informed, know where to go for information and how to put the pieces together. It's critical. You
have to know what Social Security is doing; you have to
know if you have a pension; you have to keep questioning.
You can't just say, 'Oh, I have a pension; I worked for Corporation A and I've got a pension.' You need to know how
that pension is invested. You need to know if it's pre-funded
for when you retire so there are no surprises. Well, there are
always surprises, but I think arming yourself with knowledge deserves more emphasis than planning."

PAT: "The average man's pension is usually twice that of a
woman's."

BETTE: "One of the big things over in Europe now is the age
difference for retirement. It's age sixty for women and sixty-
five for men, and there's a lot of controversy over whether
this should stay this way or not. And in Japan a couple of
years ago, a pension scheme was hatched where they
changed the laws and, at whatever age the man retired, the
wife got half the pension. All of a sudden, the late-life

divorce statistics in Japan went right through the ceiling and the authorities couldn't figure out why. It turned out that these divorces were the result of arranged marriages. These women had taken care of these men for all these years and when they finally got their half of the pension, it was *sayonara*.

"In America, divorce after fifty is one of the major financial problems facing women. It's so serious that we [AARP] had to develop a pension and divorce clearinghouse for questions because most older women go into divorce not knowing that their husband's pensions can be an asset. Most lawyers don't know that, either."

PAT: "Women must concern themselves with retirement provisions in the event of the death of the husband. I know of a woman whose husband, a teacher, handled all the finances. His choice in retirement was to take the 'optimum-until-death' option offered by his plan, which has an automatic and immediate cut-off following the death of the retiree. No funds are paid to the surviving spouse. Well, two weeks after he retired he dropped dead. His wife was left with nothing, not even Social Security, as teachers in California are not covered. She was devastated."

Talking about death, like talking about money, also doesn't happen often for women over fifty. But being prepared for death is another kind of safety net. Wills should be in place. A durable power of attorney for health care which leaves instructions specifying one's wishes for medical interventions should be on file with your doctor, your lawyer, and the people you've designated as your decision-makers.

GINNY: "I've noticed in my work that people not only don't talk to each other about death, they don't talk about making a will, about what type of service one wants, about how you want your remains to be handled. So I initiated just such a dialogue with my husband, and it wasn't easy, but in the end we pulled it all together. We took care of our wills, which we had not done; we each wrote a letter to each of the kids and put it away—his in his office and mine in my file. It is so good to feel that if something happens to Dean, I can reach for the file and the answers are there; it's already done—and visa versa. It's his last demonstration of love for me and it's my last demonstration of love for him."

DENISE: "I think there's another aspect to that; it also says to your spouse, 'I know you'll be all right.' They will remember that."

CATHERINE: "People do many things that are future-oriented but that we misunderstand because we call them 'planning.' People balk at writing their wills because they say, 'I don't want to plan my death.' But having an appropriate, valid will in line with current laws is something you must do now. It's a maintenance activity. The same thing is true of medical exams. You don't get a medical exam because you're planning to have cancer, but because you're planning *not* to have cancer. You do those things because they are long-term maintenance activities. It's really important to emphasize that the dialogue about death is a dialogue about life."

BETTE: "It's creating a safety net, so you can bungee jump off the bridge if you feel like it. You're creating an individual safety net, not a community or a class safety net. And wouldn't you feel better about jumping into something new if you knew that safety net was there?"

## BODY, MIND AND SPIRIT

*"We, as owners of this house—the chapel of the body—have to become attuned to all of its operations so that we can foster it into this new phase...."*

Our safety net discussion assumes that one is vigorous and strong. Realizing that physical well-being determines the scope of what one does with the 'gift of time,' our focus shifts to discussing preventive health measures, and to new medical protocols that are female-specific.

GAIL: "I'd be interested to know what you think women are most likely to die from; what's the number-one killer for women?"

HARRIETT: "What I call degenerative conditions. Something breaks, something happens…a deterioration that eventually leads to heart failure."

JANE: "The National Institutes of Health will be conducting a six-hundred twenty-five million dollar clinical investigation probing the causes of disease and death in mid-life and older women. Called the Women's Health Initiative, it's been described as 'The Mother of All Trials.' The NIH believes heart disease, cancer, osteoporosis, and depression are the major causes of death and disability in older American women."

BETTE: "AARP reports that studies show women are being prescribed for on the basis of research done only on men. Overall, women have poorer health than men, according to the NIH's Office of Research on Women's Health. Women live longer, but have more acute and chronic conditions than men."

GAIL: "There isn't much money for pharmaceutical companies to carry out research in preventive medicine as opposed to curative medicine. Yet the number of doctors who have started practices in alternative medicine is probably growing…this whole mind, body, spirit connection is very much a part of what they're trying to practice. Almost nothing of what they do is reimbursable. That's fine for people who have the luxury of planning ahead to prevent degenerative illnesses later by spending $1,000 now for consultations and the best vitamins and the best this and that. There are still a few states that don't even reimburse for mammograms. Imagine trying to get bone-density measurements!

(Osteoporosis is one of the three major degenerative diseases for women.) There are inexpensive ways of getting bone-density measurements, by using equipment that's fairly cheap, but it's not reimubursable by insurance companies."

GINNY: "At the Institute on Human Aging in Los Angeles, we're finding through well-documented research, that if people can get in touch with themselves, they can control these degenerative diseases. The 'miracles' that occur as a result of their psychoneural and immune systems working together successfully is that they can control and even overcome some terrible chronic ailments."

HARRIETT: "I want to listen to, and be open to something like that, but I am also a little uncomfortable. A woman with cancer can become prey to people saying, 'If you just get into my program of optimism, special diet, and positive thinking, you'll solve cancer.'"

GAIL: "We, as owners of this house—the chapel of the body—have to really become attuned to all of its operations so that we can foster it into this new phase (which I'm calling "maturesence"—adolescence being its opposite) so that when we come out on the other side of menopause, we are strong and fit and set to go for a good long stretch, into our eighties at least. How do you feel about that term maturescence?"

CATHERINE: "My word association doesn't relate it to adolescence, but to obsolescence and senescence. It's a very small family of words with that suffix. So when you produced it in that context, I immediately went to the other two rather than the mirror image of adolescence. Now if you were discussing the life cycle and had already set it up, it would work. But otherwise you have problematic associations."

GAIL: "Right. I would definitely have to set it up as a mirror image of adolescence."

GINNY: "I'm thinking of a piece of fruit. When fruit is mature, there's nothing to do with it but let it rot. It's too ripe."

CATHERINE: "Look at the vocabulary of wine and cheese instead."

HARRIETT: "It seems to me that there is something about quality of life that we should get at when we think about decline. There's a shape to life and a point at which life will end. Many of us hope that it will be quick and dignified at the end. And we're very concerned about the quality of life, too, as long as possible. There's a wonderful book by Robert Butler, *Why Survive?* (Harper & Row, 1975). He closed with a wonderful quote about the fact that to the very end of life, everyone has the right to make the most of whatever life one has...something like, 'My quality of life is what I can make of it.' We haven't put a cap on women's ages; we're really saying, 'As long as we're here.' So I think we need to think of the quality of our entire life-span when we talk about preventive therapies aimed at helping us."

MARY LOUISE: "We should be honest and frank about what aging actually feels like. There are infirmities to be contended with. Younger women should know what's coming—that it's going to change aspects of what they do and how they do it, and they should know to plan for contingencies. There will be serious illnesses and/or physical deterioration. They're going to be there, even if they don't believe it now, and it's going to cost money."

PAT: "A good general-practice doctor or internist is a must. And an annual physical will pick up adult-onset diabetes (Type II diabetes), high blood pressure, and other symptomless diseases that need control. Of course we all know that breast self-examinations, annual mammograms, and PAP smears are critical after fifty. And health insurance to supplement Medicare is also important for peace of mind. Sometimes a woman's health insurance goes down the tubes when her husband dies, if she's on his medical plan.

"Let's talk also about older women and depression. I

recently read that a depressed mood is very common among older women and that they don't know how to recognize it and do something about it. Ellie, you're our resident psychologist. What do you say?"

ELLIE: "Depression often happens for good reason. It comes during transitions in people's lives. Depression often hits first at puberty. Our culture tells us to attract men. Men want women who say, 'Aren't you wonderful!' There's a damping down at menstruation, pressure to accept a restricted role. There's good reason to be depressed: girls are being asked to give up a lot. Another flashpoint is postpartum depression, and another is when husbands become unfaithful. Women rarely have support systems to sustain them through these times. If they've had problems in childhood, these problems are re-awakened in the next transition."

She went on to describe the signs of serious (but treatable) depression, which can last two weeks or longer: 1) gain or loss of weight; 2) sleeping too much, sleeping too little; 3) feeling either slowed down or speeded up, such as hyper-anxiety; 4) poor short-term memory, lack of concentration; 5) feelings of sadness; 6) loss of appetite for everything; 7) thoughts of death or suicide.

PAT: "A lot of women who are depressed are ashamed to be feeling that way. They feel it's their own fault. The roles they have been trained to play are no-win situations: perfect daughter, perfect wife, perfect mother. The woman always finds herself at odds with what she is expected to be and what she wants to be."

SALLY: "All kinds of depression are being thrown into the pot here. My first husband suffered from clinical depression and eventually killed himself. Clinical depression is different from situational depression—which is what we're talking about here."

PAT: "A wonderful way to understand the two is to read Colette Dowling's book, *You Mean You Don't Have To Feel This Way?* (Bantam Books, 1992.) It explains how depression works on the brain and how proper medication prescribed by a psychiatrist can help. Another excellent book is *Listening to Prozac* (Penguin Books, 1993), by Peter D. Kramer."

When we go more deeply into the subject of depression, one fourth of the participants speak of either personally having gone through nervous breakdowns, (clinical depression), or of having had children or husbands go through it.

[Treatment of depression often results in a prescription for Valium, or self-medication with other drugs or alcohol. Neither is appropriate. In an interview conducted by Group 4 with a Monterey Peninsula psychiatrist, the doctor confirmed that alcoholism is a tremendous hidden problem with older women. Their doctors tend to ignore it until the liver has deteriorated beyond repair. The idea seems to be, "Oh well, after all, she's over the hill anyhow and what can you do about an old alcoholic—they're too hard to treat." Alcoholism can bring on depression and depression brings on alcoholism.]

GWEN: "I'm involved with geriatric training. The geriatrician takes fewer patients and is specifically trained to treat older people, and deal with depression."

LIBBY: "How do you find a geriatrician? How many are there?"

GWEN: "In the first year that the exam for Certification of Added Qualifications in Geriatrics was given, nine thousand doctors took the exam. Just half passed and got a license to practice in this field. They have post-residency training, and they have to have an internal or family-medicine background, and, of course, have passed the Boards. Call your area Agency on Aging for a list in your area. Their training

focuses on chronic illnesses—incontinence, falling, dementia, and depression."

ILENE: "What about Alzheimer's? Isn't that what used to be
called senile dementia?"

GWEN: "True in general. Alzheimer's is the most common form
of dementia. Another common form is multi-infarct dimentia which is caused by a series of little strokes. Psychiatrists
who take the exam for the geriatrics certification can treat
dimentia patients with greater skill and understanding."

JANE: "They're called gero-psychiatrists. They often do group
therapy for women, even with eighty- and ninety-year-olds;
these women need to know they're not alone and the
groups have proven to be great for them."

MARILYN: "I think what Margaret Fuller said in the nineteenth
century, that the best thing you could say about an older
woman was how well she was preserved, is something we
have to question today. If our assumption is that the most
we can do is to hold on to something that we had before,
you're bound to be defeated. You're not going to have the
red hair of your twenties or the unlined face of your thirties
or whatever. I think you have to go beyond preservation."

CATHERINE: "There has to be a moment when, instead of trying to hang on to youth and whatever your role was as a
young woman, you affirm and grasp and create something
new. Otherwise it really is just all downhill. And that's why
I think, with the long life cycle we have, you're going to
find that the capacity to grasp old age positively is highly
correlated with people who seize middle age, or grasp what
I've been calling a second adulthood. For women, it is absolutely critical to take control. Because so many women
have been controlled, or have followed through on earlier
decisions and commitments that have determined the
course of their lives in the past, taking control is essential.
In order to make a decision as an adult, you need to say,

'I've been an adult; I've been a successful adult. I'm going on now to start a new stage.' And it could be a state of withdrawal. It could be a state of more introverted activity or meditation. But to affirm that transition seems to me very important...then being able to make the decisions and preparations for the transitions that will come."

### RISK MANAGEMENT: TAKING THE LEAP

*"There is no chronological limit to when you can try something new."*

HARRIETT: "I want to talk about the risk-taking I think older women have to be willing to do. It doesn't necessarily mean to run for office at sixty, although many women are doing just that and politics is better for it. I've noticed many older women don't even think about taking another leap."

BETTE: "...just when they should really consider exercising all their options."

HARRIETT: "Exactly. I want to emphasize the importance of what I call "opportunistic actions" that we might want to describe as mid- or late-life risk-taking. I've noticed in many women that if they've done it once, then when they're older, they don't think twice about trying it again. It's important insofar as it reflects their optimistic view...that there is no chronological limit to when you can try something new."

RUTH B.: "The more we take risks, the more we step out there and do things, the more likely other women will be willing to do it."

DENISE: "Aren't people who take risks the kind who simply take them thinking, 'Well, somehow this will work out?' And people who *don't* take risks don't do it because they are naturally inclined to play it safe?"

BETTE: "Maybe 'risk' is the wrong word. Maybe it should be 'exercising options.'"

GINNY: "But risk is a very important part of it because if you have fear…it's like going back to school at seventy years old; there is a risk involved…the things that come to mind are competition with younger people, learning to use computers, taking tests. There's a risk to your ego. It can be psychological or financial. So I want to argue that risk is a very important word for us and that out of a potential risk will come potential options."

BETTE: "You're ready to risk because you've charted what's going to happen if X happens, or Y happens. You're suddenly saying, 'Well, now I've taken care of all those things so I'm free to go off to China if I want to. Or I'm free to take a course.'"

PEGGY: "Are you saying, 'Clear the desk by doing this or that so that you can go through the surprising doors that open and then take the risk because there's nothing in the way?'"

BETTE: "Yes…because you've armed yourself with the knowledge of where the resources are to go find the answers."

MARILYN: "Some of the advantages, and actually the values that we're espousing for this time of life are flexibility, openness, adaptiveness, change, rather than closing down or becoming fossilized. That's something I certainly can get my teeth into and hold on to and support. But we've known women who, when they hit fifty or sixty, seem to be stopped, frozen in time and frozen usually in their worst traits. That's what I noticed when I went back to my college reunion. We were all the same but *more* of what we had been originally. There was one person who had been a bit rigid and uptight (when I walked towards her I was afraid she'd have a stroke), but I realized that her reaction was just an exaggeration of what she had been. So I think that both things are at work: that the original impetus of the temperament does seem to become magnified at a certain age. But if we're here as advocates for older women, what we're saying to them is—just as in the same sense we know we have to keep our bodies flexible through exercise and yoga—we're saying that our minds have to stay flexible as well."

CATHERINE: "There's another conclusion I see emerging here. After all, remember we're talking about a thirty-seven year span in this group, and we sometimes flutter back and forth between talking about the end of life and menopause. For some of us, the new beginnings, the new taking control, the new assessments and affirmation that menopause brings, may turn out to have a very critical relationship to what we are then able to do as we age. In other words, I would disagree that you're talking about a single sweep from what you were like in college. What we've been talking about in this room, are women who, when their children grew up, took a new breath, learned some new skills, worked out, remarried in some cases."

ILENE: "You and Marilyn are both right. Some women remain stuck and some don't. We're trying to find out how to help the ones who *are* stuck. And, who knows? Some who are stuck may be perfectly happy being stuck. They may not expect or want any more out of life."

GINNY: "How do we motivate or make people feel comfortable with taking risks? A woman I met wanted to go back to college and was lamenting, 'I'll have to study, to take exams, to compete, and by the time I get out I'll be forty years old!' I said, 'Well, you're going to be forty anyway.'"

BETTE: "I would not like to sit down and say, 'Well now in five years I'm going to do X and in six years I'm going to do Y.' I think it's more about assembling the knowledge to know where to go and what you need to do to take care of crises in your life. Or even to take care of not only crises, but to take care of things in your life that need to be solved as they come up."

CATHERINE: "I really want to encourage you to say something

like risk management or risk choice. I think when you say risk-taking, it means doing something you're afraid of doing. The reality is that the people who can do what we're calling 'taking risks' are the people who have established a certain basic security within themselves and have addressed their fears. In other words, a lot of what you see in older people is that they are not making provisions and plans because they are afraid to think about the next stage. So, there's an odd sequence where you address your fear because you have to, in order to plan and provide security for the next step.

"But what we mainly mean, I think, by risk-taking is the willingness to try something new. We're not talking about skydiving: we're talking about experimentation, exploration. It might include skydiving but that should not be the main example. We're talking about what it takes to go and sign up for a class, join a program at the local church, ride a bicycle. The kind of risk-taking that gets beyond fear of something new."

RUTH A.: "I think it's the same thing as problem-solving. I think risk-taking and problem-solving are pretty much the same thing because if you're working on a problem and solving it you're taking a risk. It's a risk because the answer is not there."

MARILYN: "Well, I see them as being a little different...."

RUTH A.: "I mean, if you teach the technique of problem-solving, then risk-taking becomes easier for anyone to do. I think you need to first learn how to solve problems and then you're not afraid to go out."

CATHERINE: "I've been involved in a certain amount of discussion about risk-taking during adolescence that I got drawn into because of AIDS. There are the discussions that glorify risk-taking: 'nothing ventured, nothing gained.' But, when we talk about adolescents, we tend to talk about getting them to avoid all risky behaviors: never try a cigarette, never try alcohol, never become sexually active. What people don't discuss, usually, is the fact that we have to learn the *management* of risk. That's where you see problem-solving and risk-taking meet. And this is how you limit danger without locking yourself up at home. None of us stays home permanently for fear that a piano will be dropped off a scaffold. It could happen, but it's one of those risks that we decide not to worry about."

MARILYN: "There's a real change in attitude since my mother's generation when women were told to act their age, which meant to act in a way that's appropriate. Acting your age meant, first and foremost, not taking risks. There was conformity, a model of constraint, and even fear. Now we're here thinking that risk-taking has a value—particularly for older people. Now we're telling children and adolescents that they shouldn't be taking risks and we're telling older people, 'You're free to take a risk.' I find that a very, very interesting switch at this point."

CATHERINE: "When your children have grown up, you do, in a new way, own yourself. You belong to yourself. You take a new kind of responsibility for yourself, for your health, and financial planning. I think there's a direct connection between how you welcome menopause and your capacity to affirm and plan for the rest of your life."

JANE: "It's not about what we know, but about what we don't know. Every time I succeed in a risk, I take a breather. Risk means growth to me."

JUDITH: "Good point on taking a breather. Nothing grows all the time—except cancer."

VIRGINIA: "I would think that Sylvia, who has dived, untethered, deeper into the ocean than any human, might be our champion risk-taking role model. Aren't you ever afraid when you dive into the depths of the dark sea?"

SYLVIA: "Oh, yes, but not to the extent that I am when I step into a car and set out down the freeway with nothing between me and an oncoming car but a small, fine line. In diving you calculate all the risks before going down."

It seems a fitting last word on the subject of adventurous pursuits.

# CHAPTER EIGHT

# Passing It On

The women drifted off to bed to the sound of the gentle lapping of a turning tide. But the four of us huddled, wide awake, around the kitchen table, anxious that only one day remains before our forum is over. Have we covered everything? We explore holes in the dialogue, marshal our collective memory to pinpoint digressions, and fine-tune generalities into specifics. Over a second cup of coffee, we realize what's missing. We need to talk about how we will pass the word on to women of all ages. We review the past week and distill what has been said into a handful of characteristics that mark our group.

Early in our conversations, we called ourselves the "bridge generation." Now it's time to examine the claim. We need to talk about the ways in which each of us received information from the generation ahead of us; how we, in turn, are passing advice on to the generation that follows. Is the New Older Woman a new kind of role model for her daughter? Is she transmitting messages more openly, encouraging a sense of expansiveness and unlimited potential? We begin by drawing on our own personal experiences.

The next morning, a little before nine, shading our eyes

from the bright morning sun streaming into our circle, we begin with some generalizations on mentoring.

CATHERINE: "To be in your seventies now is to embark on a truly uncharted sea. Growing up we had so few to point the way, to pass on what was possible for older women."

GAIL: "I agree...I think it's essential to have images of those who have gone before us, exceptional women like Catherine's mother, anthropologist Margaret Mead, to understand what kept them vital and what gave them that sense of aliveness."

MARILYN: "Most women of our generation are motivated by just such a desire to pass something better along to their children, to students, or to society. That's a very large part of what is happening to us as we grow older."

GAIL: "Exactly. It's tied up with civic upbringing. Most of us grew up thinking you should give something back...I'm concerned that that's one of the things being lost in this country."

MARILYN: "And we need to transmit a sense of family history, to pass on the collective memory of our time. Women's memoirs pass on history in a different way than men's autobiographies. There is an historical void in women role models. In 1976 I was asked to review the *Norton Anthology of World Literature* from the Renaissance to the present. And I read it, all two thousand pages. When I got to the end of it I had this absolutely terrible sinking feeling that there wasn't a single woman writer. Not one. I got so angry. It was one of two experiences that made me become a feminist. And then I looked at the editorial board and it was made up of men. So who do you think is defining Western culture?"

ILENE: "But is it really fair to say we are the generation where mentoring took hold among women?"

ELLIE: "Yes, mentoring first became popular in the 70s. We

discovered that women could bond…it was a revolutionary way of thinking."

MARY LOUISE: "We didn't always label it as mentoring, but it existed."

CATHERINE: "Right. We needed to feel part of a women's cohort that was inventing and passing on a new way of being…we needed to be part of a bridge."

HARRIETT: "I experienced that sense of linkage when my mother died; you suddenly become the older generation. Then you realize in a very dramatic way that our children are our first immortality. You suddenly become conscious of being that vehicle for passing knowledge on. A personal sense of heritage often begins to inspire us, whether it's helping change the laws of government, the lives of people, writing a book, or selling an idea. We need to feel we've done something with our lives, that we've had an impact, been a part of preserving something valuable from generation to generation."

VIRGINIA: "Can we honestly say we were the generation 'on watch' during an authentic transition from limited options for older women to one where we have a sense of a second shot at life?"

CATHERINE: "Just look around you. It struck me when I read the resumes of everyone in this room. Group 4 has brought together at least one hundred people for the price of twenty-two. There is so much life experience around this circle, a tremendous common ability to adapt to change and to learn from it."

PEGGY: "Then let's tap into that collective sense. Could we each have reached this point, would we be here in this room, without mentors? Who encouraged us to 'push the envelope' of what was considered possible? In turn, do we feel the need to guide and support other women? Adding our stories together, is it fair to call ourselves The Bridge Generation?"

## ONE-ON-ONE MENTORING

*"The sharing of life experiences is an important part of mentoring…"*

Around the circle we begin recalling our guides—telling our own stories.

BETTE: "My father was my mentor. I always describe my life as backing into everything I've ever done. But I couldn't have done it if he hadn't opened doors for me. I was brought up like a son; he said I thought like a man, and that was the highest praise. Now I spend my time mentoring the kinds of women who aren't sitting here in this room…those I call the 'silent generation,' those who are afraid to ask for anything."

DENISE: "When you said that, Bette, I remembered my mother-in-law used to say of someone she admired, 'Now, that woman had a good father,' and I knew exactly what she meant. It was said with envy. I often think the same thing. I see a woman who stands straight, doesn't lean outside of herself, gives a sense of a strong, fixed center, and I think, 'That woman had a good father.' I confront the problem of my father with every authoritarian figure I meet. I know I do this, and it's given me a certain drive, but it hasn't made me confident inside myself and I'm envious of those who are. I have had maybe thirty or forty mentors in my life. Mostly men. I'm an older sister and I teach like a duck swims. I'm sure I sometimes cause pain in the process. I remember our rabbi saying, when I was a small girl, 'I am the mentor of this congregation and, on occasion, its tormentor.' I think that sometimes I *have* to be a tormentor to be a mentor."

RUTH A.: "My mentor was also a man—Buckminster Fuller. I asked him what I should do with my life and he replied, 'Well, Ruth, the world is your oyster and you can be the pearl. You can grow, you can agitate the sand so you can become that pearl.' Now women come to me and ask, 'How can I be a mother and have a career too?' And I try to encourage them to do just a little bit of everything as they can fit it in, the way I have...to raise a family and at the same time to satisfy the ego."

HARRIETT: "My father was a very handsome, outgoing man. I adored him but I really modeled myself after my mother. She did not work outside the home but she was a real achiever, a nationally ranked tennis player who also threw the javelin. In our dining room there was a cabinet and it wasn't filled with their best silver, it was filled with all the trophies she'd won. And so I had this image of a woman as *somebody*. You could do anything you wanted to. I think I felt there was some sense of being driven—driven to be a real, competitive tomboy. If I fantasized at all it was that I'd be Tom Sawyer, not Nancy Drew. I think, without dwelling on it, I began a pattern then of being a barrier-breaker for women."

GAIL: "The tomboy image speaks to me....it was a legacy from my parents, the role of the overachiever. I'm just now beginning to confront that image. It goes back to a picture of a little kid who, at four or five, is racing against the gun with six-year-old boys. They were very good training for being competitive in a world hostile to women. Now I'd like to recover my playful rebellious ten-year-old boyish side. The playfulness somehow got lost in the sense of competition."

MARY LOUISE: "Like Harriet, I lived by the example of a long line of strong women. As I've said before, they wouldn't have called themselves feminists, but they were. They didn't have the proper vocabulary but their instincts were good. I never had the proper labels either. I simply followed their example."

GWEN: "My mother was strong too. She had wanted to be a doctor but met discouragement everywhere. She was simply not 'uppity enough' to talk feminist language."

MILDRED: "Both my parents were my role models. They never said I couldn't do what I wanted to do. That's what I call good mentoring."

CECELIA: "That's the key. My mentors were all the people who said, 'You can do it.' With that message I had the feeling that no matter what I tried, it would be okay. Having internalized it, I was able to do a great many things on my own. Now I've formed two groups to mentor younger women. I love being a guide."

JANE: "That's the kind of mentoring I do. Having lived through crises, you can help others get through. At forty-eight I began to open up and tell others about my severe depression. They realized I knew what pain was. This sharing of life experiences is an important part of mentoring, the chance to identify with another person."

CLAIRE: "The mentor that had the most impact on me was a woman museum director trained at the Sorbonne. She was Grace McCann Morley, and at that time she was the most important curator west of the Museum of Modern Art in New York. She brought French culture to San Francisco. I am proud to claim her as my role model. She was always encouraging. Now my home in Venice, California, is always full of young people seeking guidance. I delight in that."

ELLIE: "My mentor was a consummate politician. I just watched her operate...she taught me more than all the books I've read. When she came to me for something I always gave it to her. That's important...mentoring is reciprocal. Now I explain to those I mentor, 'I cashed in chips for you, now you have to do the same for me.' What young women fail to understand is that mentoring is like a poker game…they have to ante up when it's their turn."

JUDY: "I was mentored by a man. There were simply no women to help. Now I'm in a position to give other women a leg up, to help them get jobs. And I delight in it. Marlene Saunders, the first woman network anchor in the nation, had to start from scratch. She feels passionately about helping other women break down the prejudice against an aging face on the news desk."

JUDITH: "In modeling there *were* no role models. There were isolated women who helped me over short periods of time. To me, mentoring means a longer span of time. I have given lots of advice over the short haul…I try to stay in touch but most beginners give up. Those who stick it out give me occasional feedback, checking in at regular intervals. To me that is not a real mentoring situation…these are simply helpful conversations."

CATHERINE: "I'm sitting here puzzled by what we mean by mentoring. I think we should be careful about identifying or equating good parenting with mentoring. We may lose some important distinctions. I was very fortunate as a child…I had lots of adults that played surrogate parents. But, to me, that is different. I don't feel I can mentor my daughter. I would reserve the word mentor for use in a work context."

DENISE: "I disagree. Why must the word be limiting? You might find that a teacher in high school was more important than anyone in your whole career."

CATHERINE: "The word mentor means teacher. We can let it mean what we want but it really should be limited to the kind of teaching that helps one function in an organizational structure."

VIRGINIA: "What about the women you devoted so much of your last book *(Composing A Life)* to?"

CATHERINE: "I think of them as contemporaries. I don't think of any one of them as a mentor in the sense of guiding me. I think of them as being part of a two-way relationship."

PEGGY: "Let's talk about institutional mentoring, whether it be in school or career: about how we learn, live by, and pass on the rules of the game."

## TEACHING THE RULES OF THE GAME

*"It means teaching the ropes...getting help from an 'old gals' network"*

CATHERINE: "Mentoring is really about working with the system: what the real rules are as opposed to the published rules, who you need to have contacts with. This is true in every system. Women go in and they know the public rules, they know how the system is supposed to work but they haven't been told how, in fact, to function in the reality of that system."

JANE: "Now I understand why you insisted we distinguish between parenting and mentoring. Mentoring means teaching the ropes...getting help from an old gals' network."

CATHERINE: "I admit, there are parents who can mentor, if they are in the same profession. But most don't know the specifics. Who is the key person on a critical committee? How does the academic world of tenure really function? How does a large corporation deal behind closed doors? Most young women go into careers and they think they're advancing splendidly, and then they find that they come to a dead end. They've hit the ceiling and there's nowhere to go...they are put on hold. They have to know where the quiet power is hidden. It's critical in the academic world, the business world, the political arena. As Harriett has said, a very large function of the National Women's Political

Caucus is mentoring, tutoring aspiring women politicians about how to raise money, and getting to know the personal needs and vulnerabilities of powerful committee chairs."

PAT: "You feel strongly that mentoring and teaching are entirely separate functions?"

CATHERINE: "Yes. I teach substantial numbers of young women every year, and most drop by my office to talk about what's happening in their lives, about decisions they have to make. I would say that the number of young women I mentor, in the sense I would like to use that word, is much smaller than that. I'll give you an example of mentoring. There's a young colleague with whom I have lunch about once a month; I try to teach her how things get done in a university. That kind of passing on of the real rules is invaluable. One example of a secret rule: until I was sitting as Dean of the Faculty at Amherst College making tenure decisions, I hadn't heard the phrase 'refereed journal.' The men knew; I didn't. Knowing that is critical in the academic world if you want to advance, because often they don't judge you by all your publications; they consider only those journals that use a referee system. If I send an article to the *Atlantic Monthly*, a clever editor will decide whether to publish it. But if I send it to *Anthropology* they will send it out to a review committee of my peers who will anonymously give a professional evaluation. That's the *only* type of publication you will get credit for when you come before the tenure committee. It may seem trivial but, I assure you, it's vital."

DENISE: "And these are the kinds of rules the senior male academics will tell the younger men but they don't tell the younger women?"

CATHERINE: "Exactly....Nobody gave me that kind of practical mentoring. What I'm trying to say is, this is part of the rules of the game. And nobody explained to me that if you publish a new idea or give a paper at a conference, you have to do it four or five times before it belongs to you. One publication doesn't float. I've had lots of valuable ideas but I simply published them and moved on…they were lost to me."

HARRIETT: "These are the kinds of rules women in politics have to understand…I call it 'institutionalized mentoring.' Women who are experienced, who have been out on the front lines, have to do it to hold on to gains and be able to move forward. It helps us withstand the inevitable backlash."

MARY LOUISE: "When I started out in politics, there were no women up the ladder to mentor me. Men were my models; they taught me the ropes. In return, I gave loyalty and credit for my successes. I think I made them proud. Now I feel a real obligation to help women overcome barriers. Even with the guidance of powerful men, I would never have become the Republican chair without the support of women. A determined cadre of three women pros, all seasoned hands, took me under their wings and showed me the ropes. At the 1968 convention in Miami we four were in on the bottom of the women's movement within the party. I remember I was reluctant to appear on TV, and I said to one of the women, 'My heart talks to me…I am with you but I just can't do it'. One of the them replied, 'You cannot be freed till every woman is freed.' I'll never forget it; that remark changed my life. Now I am in a position to help other women, and I do."

ILENE: "Did you mentor before you became a nationally recognized political figure?"

MARY LOUISE: "The word wasn't even in my vocabulary. Neither was 'empowerment' or 'vulnerability.' Remember, my career didn't start until I was sixty. It was then I began to build a platform and be strong enough to reach out to other political women. I enjoy passing on the rules, and it's not always in my own field. To me, it's not always a question of helping someone advance within your own institution. It should have more range than that."

PEGGY: "It's true, politics has proven to be one of the toughest careers to crack. As Senator Nancy Kassebaum put it, 'I found no women when I walked on the Senate floor for the first vote. I lived isolated in a world of men and I was dependent on them to guide me. Now I can share the rules of the game with other women.'"

IRENE: "In earlier days, I helped women get jobs in Washington, D.C., but as the numbers grew into a flood of women, I just couldn't keep up. One could spend one's whole life mentoring newcomers. I tried to institutionalize the process, offering brownbag lunches, telephone encouragement. Still, I found I was running a small think-tank...I would get hundreds of letters a week asking for help... I simply couldn't answer them or return all the phone calls. I was forced to rethink the process. Now I do 'one shot' mentoring."

ELLIE: "Don't you find this kind of thing is based on quid pro quo? As I said before, if you have been mentored, you owe things to your mentor—you owe loyalty."

IRENE: "My mentoring centers around finding women jobs. I always tell them, 'When you get that job, help someone else along. You have to pay back what has been done for you.'"

Around the room heads nod in agreement. Everyone seems to have had a similar experience. For the links in the chain to hold, mentoring needs to be an ongoing and continuing chain of advice from woman to woman.

LIBBY: "Roger Stevens, former director of The National Endowment for the Arts, helped me draw a mental diagram of the maze of government bureaucracy involved in the arts. Liz Carpenter, who was Executive Secretary to Vice President Lyndon Johnson and press secretary for Lady Bird

Johnson, mentored me, as she did so many women. She's a shrewd poker player who knows when to risk her chips and when to hoard them."

ILENE: "Liz was coming to Esalen until she realized it would overlap with the Democratic Convention. She promised to come if we did it again next year. We wanted to ask her what kind of mentoring is going on for new women in Congress. Are they being shown where the power buttons are? Is there an old gals' network in place?"

LIBBY: "I talked with Liz about this just the other day. If she were here she would say that there is safety in numbers, that as the pool of women grows, there will always be a guide to take one by the hand. We agreed that the quality of mentoring is also improving, that many of the newer faces bring with them the political skills they learned in state legislatures."

PEGGY: "In the Western Political Science Association, for example, tenure has been a major problem for women—virtually impossible in most major colleges. Women are particularly vulnerable here. Politics, after all, has traditionally been an exclusively male sport. A caucus has been created to focus on the rules of the game, to pass information along on unacknowledged barriers, on secret passwords. A safely tenured senior woman is always available to counsel in times of crisis. But most older women earned doctorates under the looming threat of an all-male dissertation committee. Their fear was very real—years of work were often undone in a matter of minutes by a single male vote."

Most of us agree with Libby's view that there is, indeed, safety in numbers and that the quality of women's mentoring is improving. Despite this positive generalization, the room explodes with very personal and painful accounts of academic horror stories. One example proves particularly powerful: it triggers an unusual but common physical response—a defensive folding of arms and an injured wince. As one of the participants explains, there is an expression in halls of learning which is rarely spoken but that strikes disgust and indignation in those who have heard about it— "Orals for orals." Put plainly, oral sex is demanded in exchange for a passing grade on the oral master's or doctoral exam. Even older women experience this particular quid pro quo. One of our group gives a painfully intimate account of such an experience; fortunately, the speaker had a mentor who intervened, a woman with a power base of her own. However, it took six years of documentation, student interviews, and committee hearings for the male professor to be removed. Our participant is haunted by the number of younger women who might have been spared disillusionment and indignity if older, more safely entrenched women had been better organized, more vocal, and seen more clearly the need for structuring a safety net. But, as she now says, "Thank God I had a mentor who cared, came to my rescue, and saw the judicial process through."

MARILYN: "I can identify with that sense of disillusionment. I had wonderful women teachers in high school and college who believed in me and pushed me along. In graduate school all my professors were male...that was at Harvard, Columbia, and Johns Hopkins. They were marvelous professors, top of the line. But when I went to get a job none of them helped me. I was married, I had children, I wasn't worth it. Women of our generation were not taken seriously."

IRENE: "I just want to mention that things are very gradually improving. Most professional women's organizations now have caucuses that keep a list of graduate students so that when jobs come up they are contacted. Most universities have created a more institutionalized means of communicating complaints and documenting cases of harassment.

But such stories need a public airing. It revitalizes the women's movement, especially for younger women who take the gains for granted."

JANE: "It is also disappointing to watch women who fail to mentor. I had a dean who was in a position to make a difference for women. But she refused to mentor. Her rationale : 'I had to keep my head above water to simply hold my place in a male environment…it sapped all my energy.'"

There's a buzz around the circle. Two theories about this problem surfaced: the "queen bee syndrome"—the queen who shuns potential protégés to reduce competition and longs to be co-opted by the dominant male power structure in order to feel secure, and tokenism—token members of any organization, for instance female cadets at West Point, who use all their energy just to retain their coveted position. Every woman has a story to tell; everyone knows a 'token' who crumbled under the stress.

### RE-ENTRY: A WAY UP OR A DEAD END?

*"It's ironic to note that our educational system usually fails to help older women because they aren't worth investing in."*

Many, if not most of us, have blossomed late. We are acutely aware that re-entry is not easy; it poses special problems for the older woman.

MARILYN: "I think a lot of us came here with the hope that we could talk about what some of you have labeled 'productive aging.' So I'll just throw out the whole issue of education for older women. I think if we were making a list of things that are an advantage now for the New Older Woman, as opposed to what our mothers experienced, one would be the re-entry phenomenon. It can extend right into one's seventies and eighties. Instead of looking at older women students as liabilities, most colleges have begun to see them as advantages. It's been fascinating for me to see how Stanford has instituted a program for older women within the last four years. It's very successful and actually making money for the college. So now the admissions people are out courting older students. We can begin to think about learning over a lifetime. And I don't think that is just a marketing phrase."

GWEN: "That's a recent change. In our generation re-entry women felt like tokens. So many of us here re-entered late and found no mentors at all."

PEGGY: "Yes, it was a difficult time for both those who re-entered and the pioneers who preceded us. I worked on the re-entry faculty at Cabrillo College in California and learned that timing is everything. Older women feel shaky, tenuous, and tend to be driven by perfectionism. Their tapes keep replaying, 'You can't.' Their confidence level is low: anything less than an 'A' grade is perceived as failure. They have to be given a sense of support early on—before their first test—or you lose them. They present a challenge to a teacher, but it was the most rewarding experience of my life. One incident gave me a terrific sense of encouragement. A white-haired woman—a straight 'A' student in my Introduction to American Government class—asked me if she should run for student body president. This, in a college known for young surfing types, worried me. I didn't want her to know failure so soon. At sixty-three, she was planning on law school. The next week I came across a crowd outside the student union. There she was, vigorously debating a twenty-year-old male and surrounded by her campaign team, all re-entry women over forty. I learned a valuable lesson—never assume. She won by a landslide."

BETTE: "It is ironic to have to note that our educational system usually fails to help older women, even if they are stars, because they aren't worth investing in. Their sense of commitment is questioned. They're asked why they didn't do it at twenty-two if they were serious."

PAT: "Exactly. One is made to feel less authentic, not worthy of consideration, if raising a family or financial problems have intervened."

There is a sense of backlash, even whiplash. Why have so many re-entry programs at the community college level, lost visibility, funding, and sense of mission? How can we hold on to gains made in many areas? How can older women help to hold the line? These are the questions we need to work on.

And most of all, we need recognition that members of our generation felt trapped by society's expectations, no matter when they chose to begin a career. When we were young, as Marilyn notes, we were not taken seriously if we had family responsibilities. At midlife, as Bette points out, we were not considered good investments. It's no wonder so many of us felt devalued and discounted.

The morning's conversation leaves us disquieted. We wander off to lunch in drifting groups.

## NETWORKING: THE VITAL ECHO

*"We're doing something here that's rare...we're actually listening to each other."*

After lunch our talk turns to networking, the threads of support one needs to weave in order to form a safety net of encouragement and confidence.

HARRIETT: "The kind of support I need is often from those who can empathize with what I'm going through in public life...who have been there. That is one of the reasons I came here. I felt I would find peers who would understand.

We need to look at the kind of support systems we give one another in this second stage of adulthood."

CATHERINE picks up the thread: "I think the emphasis on networking in our generation came about because we often had to use it as a substitute for being mentored. Finding no mentor, and few people senior to us to take us by the hand, we chose contemporaries with whom we could discuss problems and who would help us piece together our personal mosaic. I reinvent myself at each new stage. I am going to have to do that at least one or two times more in my life cycle. I am going to need all of you to help me. I saw it in your resumes. There is this tremendous common expertise here in adapting to change. I need to draw on it.

"You know, twenty years ago a lot of really important moments in my development took place at conferences... small conferences where a group of people could explore new ideas, think new thoughts, spark creativity in each other. That format has almost completely disappeared. Now people appear in sequence on platforms but they're not talking to each other. Here there is a shared thread: thinking about honing one's skills for transitioning, learning things from one another that will carry over into that new stage. There is that vital echo around this circle."

BETTE: "We're doing something here that is rare: we're actually *listening* to each other. I go to hundreds of conferences...I plan hundreds of them. This just doesn't happen. Most of the time everyone talks at once or listens apathetically. I keep asking, 'Why don't women listen to each other?' The speakers may have interesting things to say but four conversations are going on at the same time. There is no real interchange. I feel very much like Catherine does...this is a chance to step back and get to know women from other fields, some a little younger, some a little older. Back in

Washington, D.C., the whole lifestyle of spending ten to twelve hours a day in your office doesn't offer one time to really get to know other women, to listen to how other women in your age group cope."

JANE: "I can relate to that. In the years I've been in the women's movement, I've felt that one of the best things we can do for ourselves is to connect with women our own age — women who will nourish us. This is what I want: people I like, sitting around a kitchen table talking. It's like a college dorm. And there are so many ways we could make this happen."

RUTH B.: "I expected to be enriched by coming here to talk to successful women in other fields...and it has been happening around that kitchen table. It feels wonderful."

CECELIA: "The idea of cross-fertilization appealed to me...it really intrigued me. And the idea was conceived by four women who themselves brought such different professional and personal histories here."

DENISE: "It's given me a chance to talk with my peers about how it is at this age. That's never happened to me before."

GINNY: "I've felt like a sponge here...soaking up how all of you have made your transitions."

MARILYN: "Not many of us can survive totally alone. Tillie Olson exploded the myth of the lone genius in her book *Silences* (Delacorte Press/Seymour Lawrence, 1978). More than men, talented older women value connections...a sense of community...a chain of friends and supporters. I think it is very unwise to neglect our women friends as so many women have done in the past. I now look at some of my close friends in ways I didn't in the past. I treasure them. When I went back to my twenty-fifth college reunion, I thought, these are women of my generation. They've had children, they've had divorces, they've had lovers, and I had this sense of bonding with them I had missed in college. I am determined to keep these friendships alive. I came here to experience this same kind of shared experience, to get a different vision. I wanted to get rid of the old model of being over fifty. I needed to get this new image by being with my peers—some a little older—who could give me a feel for what my future might look and feel like."

BETTE: "I understand what you are saying. I have a different appreciation now too. I've always enjoyed the company of men but I must say, looking around the circle, this is the company I value and enjoy."

JUDY: "Yes. I'm fifty-nine. I don't expect people to whistle at me as I go down the street. I do expect them to pay attention to my mind. What is the force that makes older women more interesting to me, why are they more fascinating, more wonderful to be with than someone younger? Because they read, they have had more experience with which I can connect. There are commonalities in what we've read, talked about, lived through. That's what defines us."

MILDRED: "Ninety-nine percent of the time, I'm the only woman talking to a lot of men. This is the first women's group I've taken time to meet with. It's an entirely new experience."

DENISE: "I enjoy the company of women now. It's been very important to me to realize, having grown up in Johannesberg where women were brought up to have babies and be nice, that there are literally a million different ways to be a woman. That's been confirmed here."

MARILYN: "But we have to be careful that, in trying to differentiate ourselves from other women, we don't end up feeling superior to them. We take the risk of cutting ourselves off from the kinds of cohort support we need."

SYLVIA: "As a scientist I'm not often in the company of women. It's not encouraged. I live out the title 'The First Woman Who...' does something. The scientific approach is sexless and that's characterized the way I've gone through life. It's what you *do* that counts, not whether you're a man or woman. This dialogue with women is all new to me... fascinating but foreign."

We all begin to imagine what mentoring and networking might mean to all of us in the future. We trip over each other as we begin to project how such support might generate energy for the projects each one of us has on the burner for the coming year.

JANE: "I think it's vital that we go from a conversation about mentoring and networking to talk about each other's work. I need to take this group's enthusiasm about our individual efforts home to my friends. I can't wait to tell them I met Claire Falkenstein...and I want to see Judy's World War II documentary. This is what older women can do for each other. It's not just getting together for a week; it's seeing how we can help each other move on our own work. And I think that has been a very neglected part of older women's concerns."

ILENE: "I like Claire's linear concept of the 'never-ending screen,' a continuous flow of ideas, an ongoing dialogue, a constant recharging of the batteries. How can we in Group 4 help you share and sustain the resources and energy that we've generated around this circle?

"But I have a problem with the term 'networking.' It's still so linked in our consciousness to the 'Old Boys' Network.' Perhaps we should just lighten up on it and put it in perspective. I have an anecdote that may help. There's what I call the Billie Byers style, which proves that women can change perceptions, not by scolding, but by humor and irony. Billie is a friend who was elected president of an important foundation. She was asked to lead a panel at a national conference of foundation leaders from across the country, and accepted the invitation with some trepidation. But she came up with a winning idea; she titled the session

'Learning from the Good Old Boys,' and when the time came, the session's billing had attracted an overflow audience, including many men. As part of the presentation, a group of women conducted a mock board meeting, mimicking male networking strategies: how they got things done. At first the audience was baffled, but soon burst out laughing. They got what the women were saying about networking on the golf course and at the club. It was a very successful technique and many of the CEOs later commented, 'We had no idea we seemed like that to you.'"

ELLIE: "I remember when the Women's Forum started up in 1972 in New York. We were very happy to be thought of as a counterweight to the old boys' network. It has, after all, tremendous power. In the Bay Area, men in prominent positions go to the Bohemian Grove and piss on the trees, and George Bush says to someone, 'Would you like to be Secretary of State?' Women are excluded. Supposedly, members are just being playful, but in reality the associations they make there creates a network through which major decisions are made. So the point is, we get annoyed that we're not in it, but what's wrong with us having one too?

"We need a women's forum where you meet people of talent and you make contacts. You yourselves are illustrating what you say and this makes you uncomfortable—mentoring, networking women's style. We're doing it right here. There can be a quid pro quo. We give Group 4 help with our imaginative projects and they provide all of us with a network. We can help each other with the imaginative projects some of us just outlined. It is, as Harriet would say, a win-win situation. It's networking...we have to learn the male systems. We are not helpless old women. We become relevant as we gain access to what's been labeled 'Male.'"

PEGGY: "I think it's positive to emulate men's networks as long as we're not co-opted into using their style. We don't have to be confrontational or 'piss on the trees' to hold our ground. We do need to hold on to our capacity to build consensus. Republican Senator Olympia Snowe from Maine put it well: 'I don't like to hurt anybody, even in politics. In a confrontaional situation I'm not interested in the game-playing and power-maneuvering that I think is more commonly associated with men than women. I still believe there is strength rather than weakness in caring and coalition building.'"

## LINKING UP — PASSING IT ON

*"More and more, I think people will want to share intergenerational lives."*

The conversation segues gracefully from cohort networking to forging linkages with the next generation of women, those now in mid-life. The women in this circle feel a desire to hand down some of their hard-won, often painfully acquired lessons. They feel a strong personal sense of generational stewardship.

Each generation would like to spare the next the need to reinvent the wheel. History tells us this instinct has been particularly acute in women. Grandaughters sit fondly at their grandmothers' knee, nod knowingly, and then insist on experimenting for themselves. We turn our attention to finding ways we might pass on any wisdom we've accumulated about this new second adulthood, this thirty-year reprieve. What did we really have to say? Would anyone want to listen? Our conversation moves first to the barriers that exist between generations.

ELLIE: "I've told younger women, 'You don't need us now and that's because you're at the height of your personal power. It's all well and good when you're younger, but wait until you move up the ladder and try to be an executive vice

president. You'll find out it's good to have a women's network, someone to go to for help.' Of course, they don't believe it will ever happen to them."

CATHERINE: "We're clearly moving in a direction where there
are going to be more and more young people resentful of
the social burden that the elderly represent to them."

GINNY: "There is a great deal of concern that the older generation will be electing the political figures, and making the
decisions about the distribution of tax dollars. The perfect
example is the trend of older people not voting for school
bonds. There is growing anxiety that those coming along
behind us, because of the sheer numbers involved, will feel
forced to wage generational battles."

BETTE: "I think it's the younger generation that is going to go
down the tubes in any generational warfare. I think a number of things are going to happen in the future: it's likely
that senior citizen discounts are going to disappear; Social
Security itself will be diminished."

GINNY: "Yes, Social Security will look very different. By the year
2000 they're going to increase the age at which you receive
full benefits to sixty-seven...most experts say it will be seventy eventually. It will probably become 'needs based,' so
younger people will be afraid to bank on Social Security
benefits. They may not be there."

PEGGY: "Three years ago I created and taught the first course in
the country on 'The Politics of Intergenerational Conflict.'
I think the results of a random survey the students did tells
us a lot about perceptions of conflict versus cooperation. I
presumed that when we analyzed the data we would find
indications of a coming confrontation. Not so...we found
that the old and the young identified with each other's vulnerabilities, and the 'sandwich generation,' caught in the
middle, had very strong feelings about trying to meet the
needs of the two extremes. There was very little sign of

hostility and a lot of cause for hope. I was surprised. My
course title was clearly misleading. It's now called 'Intergenerational Politics: The Art of Consensus Building.'"

Our thoughts turn to the ways generations depend upon
each other and are willing to lean and be leaned upon.

MARY LOUISE: "There are so many intergenerational options.
In my life I have three younger friends with whom I travel;
one is my grandaughter's age. I suspect we are so close because we bring different interests and different perspectives
to our friendship. Age becomes a positive factor."

BETTE: "More and more I think people will want to share intergenerational lives. When the baby-boom generation ages,
they will be much more comfortable with this. They won't
want to live in nuclear homes; they'll feel the isolation.
Maggie Kuhn is a role model here…insisting on living,
well into her eighties, in an intergenerational compound."

IRENE: "There's a good example of cross-generational lifestyles
in Washington, D.C. —a program designed to ease the load
on older women who take in students. It has enabled older
women to stay in their homes and, at the same time, helped
students find affordable housing. Both benefit from a sense
of connectedness."

PEGGY: "I have been intrigued by a program called Generations United, a Washington, D.C. based organization that
attempts to identify the problems of the old and the young
to see how each generation might help the other through
specific programs. I went to two training sessions designed
to showcase programs all across the country in which generations match needs and trade services. For instance,
there's a program in New York City in which teenagers deliver meals to housebound elders, and on roller skates no
less, while older women provide day care for working
mothers. There were, of course, some notable mismatches,

but on the whole the programs worked. There was a sense of generational balance. It was difficult to tell which generation gained more."

MARILYN: "And we should be talking about the kind of support we give and receive from our children. You can get so much validation from them. Years ago I said to my son that when I became an old lady I was going to kick up my heels and wear a purple hat and be eccentric. I forgot about it. About a week ago he said, 'You know, I was at a fair recently with my girlfriend, and we were looking for a purple hat for you.' Imagine, he had remembered!"

PEGGY: "When I was going for my Ph.D., I would get discouraged and my daughter would say, 'Go for it, dammit.' She has always been there, daring me to do more. She seems to know exactly when to goose me."

CECELIA: "In my study of zesty older women, I found they invariably cultivated many friends of all ages and made a point of attracting younger people to share meals, music, hobbies, and intellectual interests. They lived longer for it."

PEGGY: "I send my students in the Politics of Aging seminar out to low-income housing units to talk with older women. The first time around I warned them they might meet with hostility, suspicion, or fear. After the third week, they reported back that the women had spruced themselves up, their apartments were cheerier, cookies were waiting. They were obviously waiting for the doorbell to ring. Students kept individual journals of the experience...they began to look at some of these women as the grandmothers they never knew. They would comment, 'My God, the stories they can tell!'"

GWEN: "I had much the same experience at Stanford."

PAT: "I'd like to make the link between mentoring each other and accomplishing individual goals by throwing a challenge into the circle. Let's share our number-one priority for the next year. If we 'followed our love,' as Gail calls it, what would we want to accomplish in the next twelve months?"

GINNY: "I've been asked to be the director of an Institute on Aging…to start a whole new institute on human aging. It would involve a human ecology approach, developing a community with a communal spirit. It's based on a blending of a Japanese and a Swedish model. It's an incredible opportunity. I ask myself whether I have the energy. And I have to admit—I am scared."

BETTE: "I have been offered an opportunity to start all over again with an international activities department for the AARP. I am kind of reluctant because I think at my age I'm becoming a little lazy. But it certainly presents a challenge. One of the things I would like to do, if this works out, is to look for short-term volunteer opportunities in Eastern Europe and Latin America for older persons who cannot sign up for a two-year hitch in the Peace Corps. I'd like to go to Eastern Europe and find out what their needs are and try to match those needs to volunteers."

VIRGINIA: "To use Catherine's phrase, you'd be recycling some of your old skills."

BETTE: "Yes. I've never used them. I've two degrees in international relations, one in Soviet Studies and one in African Studies. I guess I am coming full circle. It seems fitting I should finally put these old skills to work."

CATHERINE: "Bette, you'll be a living example of one's ongoing ability to reinvent oneself. As for myself, I just signed on for the next book. It will be a three year project…a book about learning through the life cycle. So it's very relevant to all the things we've been talking about."

RUTH B.: "I have several things I desperately want to do. There is my farm for the homeless. And another of my concerns is the explosion of AIDS among teenagers. The rate is frightening in San Francisco, much higher than the numbers that are officially released. There are all these kids that are not getting any AIDS education because they've dropped out of school. I think I've devised a way of reaching them through public service tapes. The kids would actually write the script and I would get The Gap or Esprit to buy prime air time to play them. We also need an early intervention center in San Francisco, a place for people to go when they learn they are HIV-positive to obtain counseling, education, and medical help: a one-stop service where they'll be stroked and made to realize it's not as hopeless as they've been told."

CECELIA: "I want to go to Hunza and study the old women there...they live to a very old age. The men have already been researched. So I want to combine trekking, which is my hobby, with interviewing Hunza women to find out how they live. This has been a fantasy of mine and now I am going to do it."

RUTH A.: "I've been commissioned to do the sculpture for the Japanese/American internment memorial in San Jose. I'm excited about that, but my biggest passion is to establish an arts high school for the Bay Area."

MILDRED: "My real challenge is to find somewhere where I have never been and go there and then, of course, I will be going back to my beloved Amazon."

MARILYN: "Well, what I have to say may seem boring. My youngest child will be in his last year at Stanford and I want to be around for him. I worked all the time that he was a child and suddenly I realize this is my last opportunity to be next to this wonderful son who writes and directs plays. So I am not taking on any new projects this year, but I will be finishing my book, *Blood Sisters: The French Revolution in Women's Memory*."

Our time together is coming to an end. The New Older

Woman has been explored, questioned, and envisioned. We wonder, as we take leave of our new friends, if our time together will mean anything to anyone but ourselves. Will the women who came to Esalen find a sustaining inspiration in the concept we've articulated within their lives and careers and, will the examples they set inspire *new* role models?

# CHAPTER NINE

# Reflections, Connections, Continuity

As Friday arrived and the five days of dialogues drew to a close, we invited a critique of the experience from both personal and group perspectives. We started by asking participants why they had accepted our invitation in the first place, what they thought of the format, what they felt they had gained, and how the substance and spirit of the venture related to the future.

## REACHING OUT

*"Do you want our ideas of things* you *can do?*
*Is that part of the deal here? That's easy for us...."*

For Group 4, the conversations would produce twenty-five hours of audio tapes in 1991, and an equal number of video recordings in 1992. In the final hours, we asked participants to point out ways in which our experience could be used to reach out to others, or to stretch ourselves for new projects.

ELLIE took us right into it: "I'd like to see a real ongoing connection. We shouldn't forget that there's an already existing resource, the International Women's Forum, the world's largest organizational network for women of achievement in business, government, science, academia, and the arts, in Washington, D.C. It is a cohesive organization ready to go—the purpose of the Forum is really networking. Or, we could go it on our own, be the first women's group to put itself on a modem. Then we could continue our conversations and help each other with our research. It would be good for loneliness and infirmity—a mutual support group. Let's take the risk and jump into the twenty-first century!"

JANE: "Group 4 should write a book, and you should get some of the people from this conference to do workshops."

CATHERINE: "Yes, give more people a chance to think about transitioning, clearing the decks, stepping out during this gift of time. You could do seminars on the subject; you'll find echoes from one seminar to the other."

ILENE: "I'm hearing that we need to pool our knowledge and agree on a means of communicating and expanding the dialogue. I'm happy that you want to keep in touch with Group 4 and with each other. Yes, it could build."

PEGGY: "And we might think about having intergenerational dialogues—let generations really talk to each other and resonate."

MARY LOUISE: "We could pass on to the next generation what it *really* feels like to age. Younger women should know what's coming, that it's going to change aspects of what you do and how you do it."

GINNY: "Exactly. What kind of role modeling do you want to do for your daughters and daughters-in-law who are coming along?"

The suggestions were welcome. Now we wanted to hear candid reactions about the way the dialogues were structured: it was time for a reality check.

## "THE ESALEN WAY": CRITIQUING THE FORMAT

*"Coming from a string of academic conferences, I was up-tight and antsy at first: I thought we needed more structure. But we ended up learning so much from each other just because all these elements worked together to help us relax."*

GINNY: "I missed having women from other socio-economic levels with us. We need a better mix, more ethnic and cultural diversity."

BETTE: "One group that was missing entirely here: the woman who is entirely focused on being a homemaker. After all, in our generation most women fall into that category."

CATHERINE: "I don't feel at this beginning stage of the concept of the New Older Woman that you necessarily need to aim for a representative of every group. What is critical in a small starter group like this is that everyone be articulate and ready to speak up. It's been very important to me that everyone is not only here as an individual but as an expert. Later, if you want to go into a very poor community, it's not just that the problems are different, it's also that the format must change. Maybe you're not aiming at a constituency of poor women but of policy-makers. You will have to decide."

ILENE: "After some really long thought, we decided we had a stable of racehorses here who should be allowed full rein. Were we right?"

DENISE: "I feel the very informal, minimal direction given by the organizers has been very important for this group and if you had tried anything else, we would have subverted it!"

MARILYN: "This kind of place and this kind of futuristic topic dictated the open, loose format. I found at first that I was a little disoriented. I was expecting something a little less experiential, less personal. Once I got into it, I was comfortable. But then everything conspired to make the fit easy. The balance between the personal and the analytic has worked out nicely. But I couldn't have foreseen that on the first day. The setting, the cushions, the trees, and water contributed to making us all relax and speak freely. I don't know if you could have this candid a conversation in another kind of setting. Coming from a string of academic conferences, I was uptight and antsy at first: I thought we needed more structure. But we ended up learning so much from each other just because all these elements worked together to help us relax. Now I realize the value in talking in a totally informal, non-thematic way. If you asked me what was the most important thing I got out of the conference, it would be this easy and intimate connection among women which was achieved here."

PEGGY: "That strikes a bell with us, Marilyn. We liked the idea of a free-flowing, agenda-less format. But now, coming from you veterans of the professional meeting circuit, we appreciate the affirmation of that choice. Our next task is to translate the essence of our meetings into a larger audience format. We'll be working on that."

PAT: "We all offered a lot of personal stories. Did we overdo the anecdotal approach?"

CATHERINE: "Life *is* anecdotal; I think it was important."

PEGGY: "It was interesting to step back and watch how we addressed topics. I would hear those of us in Group 4 say we would like to move from the personal to the general. Then I'd hear someone just minutes later telling a personal story."

CATHERINE: "But there's a difference between the anecdote as chitchat and the anecdote as a tool. To me, an anecdote can represent the beginning point of real learning. It is valuable when someone says, 'I don't have data on this for one thousand women, but I *do* know a woman who....' That is the first step in working toward meaningful generalizations."

JUDY: "Although I don't think very often of specifics, one thought

I keep coming back to is how rare and marvelous to have a group of bright women come together to share ideas —no grades given, no reports written. I suspect that this time has energized all of us in ways that are not entirely predictable."

One final question from Group 4: *Collectively, what have you gotten out of these five days at Esalen?*

JANE: "Right at the top of the list: the wonderful people I've met here...the joy of sitting here in this room and talking about things that I've often felt very alone with. To be with such fantastic women with whom I hope to remain in touch was well worth the trip across a continent."

GWEN: "It's been an incredible experience, personally and professionally. It's been reassuring to know the resources we share. I felt a little tension as we started the week. I'm a goal-oriented academic; I want outcomes. Now, I'm totally relaxed. It was a nurturing experience."

ELLIE: "Relationships took first priority. It was wonderful to be able to share ideas candidly in this non-competitive circle. I also felt some initial tension about the end result, a Calvinist habit of mine. The discipline of my work makes it a little hard to unwind. But you got material for a book; we formed a network. Everybody wins."

JUDITH: "I had said it would take an atom bomb to wean me away from my only vacation time. I've learned so much; it's been well worth it. I leave with a vision of what older women can be. The whole experience here confirmed what writer and academic Dorothy Sayers claimed: 'Time is stopped by a younger woman, but an older woman is unstoppable.'"

CLAIRE: "I've been to several conferences but this has been the best. Meeting with women and thinking through life is the most creative and unusual thing I've ever experienced. What impressed me most was the truthfulness...no holds barred...no hiding. Let's leave remembering this: just DO IT...don't think about the end...just keep on DOING."

LIBBY: "Esalen was just the right place; it adds yeast, throws us off balance, and forces us to change our self images. No position papers, everyone on a level playing field. I arrived feeling my brain had become a sieve: now I feel it's a sponge. You've given me focus, authentication, and self-awareness about what I want to be doing. Now I'm determined to carve out the time to do it. Nixon had a phrase for it: 'The lift of a driving dream.' Instead of doing one for the Gipper, I hope to go home and do something for the Group."

SYLVIA: "I've always been the token woman scientist at male conferences. This is the first occasion for me to step away from focusing on science and into a broader context. The rules have dictated openess: come with shoes off and defenses down, all cards on the table. There's been an ease in talking about anything—dying, coping, kids coming home again, the physical process of aging. I have friends, but we don't talk about things like this. We talk *around* an issue; occasionally it unfolds into a conversation. But here I've met women who are not just taking this gift of time and coasting."

VIRGINIA: "Sylvia, you take the prize for someone coming in, throwing off your shoes, leaning back on the pillows, and immediately being yourself."

ELLIE: "That was a risk we all took—dropping in with a group of strangers. Incredibly, it worked."

GAIL: "I'd just like to say again, what I said at the beginning of the week, that I think we have hit on something really profound in these few days: that the source of continuing aliveness is identifying your love and pursuing it. It's that creative interplay of yourself in the world that no one can take away from you. This is the through-line that makes your life vital."

MARY LOUISE: "The opportunity to talk seriously about life experiences with women of your own generation who understand, share, sympathize, and critique is exciting. I know I will feel the same surge of energy, optimism, and enthusiasm when I go home and tell other women about it."

At the week's end, the Saturday departure from Esalen was bittersweet, in some ways reminiscent of the last day of summer camp. There were hugs and exchanges of addresses, consultations of schedules, promises to keep in touch, and wistful looks back at our house as it dropped from view. It was hard to close the door on the days that were isolated in time, of stress-free communication between women.

We had promised everyone an atmosphere of collegial informality, not knowing exactly what that might evoke. The trust and candor that emerged remains intact, and we *have* stayed in touch. Our doors, phones, and fax lines are open to each other. Our New Older Woman dialogues were initially undertaken in the hope that other women might share not just the substance, but the spirit of the venture, and it seems we were successful.

## THE NETWORK TODAY

*In the time that has elapsed since our two dialogues, the twenty-two participants have continued to share resources with us, some with each other, and to sustain the energy level that had brought them to Esalen in the first place. When we informed them that we were completing this book, we asked each for an update on their personal and professional scenarios.*

Only a few months after our meeting, **Ruth Asawa** wrote
to inform us that one of her dreams was almost fulfilled: the
San Francisco High School for the Arts was a near reality,
with three-hundred and fifty students enrolled. "Theater
tech students built a theater out of an elementary school
auditorium...we have vegetables growing in the garden
and grass planted," Ruth exulted. Last year we received a
note from her with the glad news: "In 1994 San Francisco
voters passed a bond issue for a new high school for the arts
in the heart of the city, adjacent to the new public library,
the symphony hall, and the opera house. We will finally
have something great to offer students."

The sculpture Ruth described when she was at Esalen,
a memorial in San Jose, California to the World War II
Japanese-American internees—was completed and dedicated in 1994. CBS Television filmed the dedication for
Charles Kuralt's *Sunday Morning* program. Ruth also received the National Women's Caucus for the Arts Award in
1993, and last year her architect husband, Al Lanier, gave
her a new studio of her own.

When **Catherine Bateson** left Esalen, she planned to
return in two months for a mother-daughter weekend seminar she would lead with her daughter, Sevanne. It was the
first outgrowth of the New Older Woman dialogue, coming
about when Esalen's Program Director, Nancy Kaye Lunney, decided to initiate more all-women gatherings. According to Catherine, the successful seminar attracted ten
mother-daughter pairs. A variety of other workshops for
women have since taken place.

Without pause, Catherine continues a busy teaching and
writing schedule, telling us of her latest publication in a recent note: "My new book, *Peripheral Visions: Learning
Along the Way* (Harper Collins, 1994), essentially deals with

learning from experience, or if you like, the process whereby experience is converted into wisdom, for a long (or exciting) life does not by itself guarantee continuing learning. Sometimes painful experiences are repressed, prejudices hardened, or events seen in isolation without on-going implications. Learning along the way requires a certain style of experiencing, a form of participant observation."

From **Ginny Boyak**, a gracious note arrived just a few days after our meetings: "Many, many thanks...the conference was superbly organized, the participants were incredibly bright, and the surroundings were beautiful. Bless each of you for the opportunity to explore this provocative subject. I have shared my experience with a number of people, all of whom are interested in the follow-up from your intense efforts." Since then, Ginny organized, and now directs, the Human Aging Institute in Santa Rosa, California, an education program she formed in conjunction with Pacific LifeCare Corporation, a non-profit adult residential development founded by her son.

During our conference, we had called them Ruth A. (Ruth Asawa) and Ruth B. (Ruth Brinker). Apart from sharing the same first name, they were close friends and had common interests in several San Francisco projects. **Ruth Brinker** has moved on to a new and stimulating project: seeking constructive employment and decent housing for homeless families with children. She found that projects for homeless people didn't interest anyone, but environmental projects did. So she repackaged an idea she had discussed at Esalen: utilizing unused city property for urban farms, where small crops could be intensively cultivated on small plots and sold to San Fransisco gourmet restaurants, thereby employing homeless families. Fresh Start Farms is a solid success. Ruth's mission is harvesting its own crop of kudos: she will receive the National Environmental Achievement Award from the Renew America Foundation and a listing in its 1995 Environmental Success Index.

We knew **Denise Scott-Brown** had found her Esalen week as far from her normal routine as a trip to outer space, and we were delighted to receive her reflections a few weeks later: "I've been thinking about the Group 4 conference as I rush around trying to catch up from my few days of doing something for *me*." She was obviously happy she took those days: "I feel I'll have something of them for the rest of my life." Denise isn't hard to keep track of; her firm's projects continue to attract worldwide interest and she is, in her own words, enjoying the privilege of a seven-day work week. "Our firm continues to grow and we are building a hotel and sports complex in Japan and a Hotel du Department in France (similar to a state capitol in the United States) and projects in New York, California, and at the University of Pennsylvania and Dartmouth, where I have happily assisted in campus planning. In retrospect, Group 4 was a wonderful opportunity to learn what it means to be an older woman (new? old?). Most of my life is led with people much younger than I, and I found it reinforcing to enjoy the company of women my age." In the interim, Denise has been awarded three prestigious medals: The National Medal of Arts (1993), The 1992 Philadelphia Award (1993), The Benjamin Franklin Medal (1993), as well as four honorary degrees. Just last week, Pat, while on a trip to London, saw Denise being interviewed about her work on the BBC.

In a recent call, **Libby Cater** said: "All those high-flying aims and inspired plans of action I formulated as I left Esalen...well, life intervened. There is a serious illness in my family. Douglass and I have been on the fringes of political life—Lady Bird Johnson's eightieth birthday party in Austin, Texas, the Renaissance Weekend in North Carolina with President Clinton and fifteen hundred other 'Friends of Bill.' Just know that it is the image of our circle at Esalen and the memory of our conversations that I use as my 'self-starter' and as my support in getting through a very difficult time."

Staying in touch with **Dr. Sylvia Earle** is akin to snagging a shooting star: her career continues to soar. Her latest book, *Sea Change, A Message of the Oceans* (G.P. Putnam's Sons, 1995), is a powerful brief for the endangered life of the seas. It opens our eyes to the magnitude of our ignorance about the ocean, the earth's largest and most crucial natural resource. She reports that she recently became a research associate at the Smithsonian Institute, and continues serving as president of Deep Sea Exploration in Oakland, California. As a role model, Sylvia serves feminism as few others have, by transcending gender through achievement and a noble passion for her vocation.

**Claire Falkenstein** is furiously busy at her Venice studio, having recently decided at age eighty-seven to take her affairs into her own hands. Impatient with art dealers, she's representing herself with more success than she anticipated and is putting together seven separate exhibitions. She also decided to simplify her life and last year sold her historic Montmartre studio in Paris. Recognition continues to come her way; she gave an oral history of her life to the University of California at Los Angeles, now in the archives of the New York Museum of Modern Art.

The further adventures of **Cecelia Hurwich** could fill a book. She fulfilled her long-held dream of trekking in the Himalayas, visiting Hunza villages, and interviewing the elder Hunzakut women. "I fulfilled my dream!" she wrote ebulliently. "There were eight of us, all friends, sharing a wonderful month of cultural experiences." She spoke at a

conference of the International Federation on Aging in
Bombay, India, and presented a workshop on "Creative
Aging" at the American Society of Aging in Chicago in
1993. She also chaired a roundtable at the International
Congress of Gerontology in Budapest, Hungary. Her latest
research project is a study comparing a population of
working-class women past seventy with her original research of upper-middle-class "Vital women in their seventies, eighties, and nineties."

**Sally Lilienthal** was looking casually elegant, as usual,
when we last met in San Francisco at her Fort Mason office, the nerve center of the Ploughshares Fund, a foundation she founded and to which she devotes a tremendous
amount of energy. Her twin passions continue to be peace
initiatives and human rights, both of which take her to conferences across the country. We had called on Sally to discuss our book and ask for pointers; we were considering
interviews with other prominent older women across the
country. Sally set us straight: "You are *not* social scientists,
you are *not* researchers. The integrity of your project is in
the material you have, from your conferences, from the
women who answered your call, and from your own perspectives. Don't *think* of messing around with it!" We are
deeply grateful for her advice in steadying our course.

**Mildred Mathias** continued to retrace her own footsteps
to wilderness areas and to teach seminars on biodiversity. A
year after the forum, she wrote, "...it has not been a good
year. My husband died while we were on the Copper
Canyon trip in Mexico, in early May, and I also lost my
favorite colleague who had accompanied me on my trips to
the Amazon."

Mildred went to Kauai to help with planning for the National Tropical Botanic Garden, which suffered major
damage from hurricane Iniki in 1992, and later spoke at a

workshop for Smithsonian Associates in Washington, D.C.

Shortly after receiving her last letter, we learned that Mildred Mathias died at her home in Brentwood on February 16, 1995. She leaves a legacy of gardens, projects for conservation and restoration, and a great body of botanical study throughout the world. Her memorial is the botanical garden at the University of California, Los Angeles, which she conceived and planted, and which was named in her honor on its completion. We were fortunate to have shared her wisdom and goodness.

**Bette Mullen** has, in Catherine's terms, recycled her skills and finally come full circle—back to her first love—languages and international politics. She is now director of international activities for the AARP, a job that has her jetting around the world 80 percent of the time. Phrasing it in professional terms, Bette writes, "I'm responsible for developing plans to serve the forty thousand overseas members in one hundred fifty-two countries who belong to the AARP, to liaison with the United Nations, to represent the Association at all international conferences, and to sponsor workshops." As such, she is the AARP's chief delegate to the United Nations.

"In just the few months since the forum, I have been in Denmark, Bali, India, Japan, South Africa, Australia, and China. When I was asked to give the keynote speech at a meeting in Portland, Oregon, on health-related issues, I found myself asking our headquarters, 'Am I allowed to travel in the States?' Donna Shalala, Secretary of Health and Human Services in the Clinton Cabinet, spoke instead." She has met with Esalen housemates in strange and wonderful places. The last was in Bombay, were she ran into Cecelia Hurwich on her way to Nepal.

When **Judith Paige** thanked us for our courage and vision, we realized her words affirmed that our original optimistic premise could be a source of strength for other women. Had we hit the mark or set something in motion that would continue to grow? Judith's words were encouraging: "You have inspired me so much. The Group 4 idea has remained with me, and recently my sister and I put together a small conference using the Esalen experience as a guide. We invited ten women and everyone was anxious to come. I think we laid the seeds for many projects on that day. One of the things the women felt they wanted to do at the end of the day was to extend the process by having each participant produce another such conference and, hopefully, for the process to continue so that many, many women could share similar dialogues."

With two book proposals in to publishing companies and the latest edition of *Hot Flash* (her national newsletter for women) behind her, **Jane Porcino** suffered a stroke in the fall of 1994. However, with her indomitable will, and the help of her caring husband, Jane is expected to be fully rehabilitated shortly. During this time, she has used her strength to continue writing. She is an inspiration to all of us who are of an age to hit one of those pot-holes in the road.

Like Libby, not everyone in our circle had been able to live out her professional passion. At Esalen, **Judy Reemstma** told us she had just committed herself to a three-year project, the production of a ten-part series on World War II to be released on PBS in 1995, the fiftieth anniversary of the end of the war. It was to be narrated by Walter Cronkite and filmed in four locations: Los Angeles; Mobile, Alabama; Brooklyn, New York; and the entire state of Iowa. She had already hired a distinguished team of producers who were to interview the men and women who spent their youth living out the story which Judy describes as "changing America forever." But now, after more than two years of "living on the edge," as she puts it, Judy reports that the project was cut off for lack of funding. Judy let her feelings show in a letter to Group 4: "I fear for the future of this institution [PBS], which has such great power to teach and enlighten. Much of corporate America is deserting, and the new Congress is leading a charge to abolish the Corporation for Public Broadcasting, the National Endowment for the Humanities, and the National Endowment for the Arts. The next few years will be critical.

"The only good thing to come out of all this is that I have had a lot more time to spend with my husband. Since the conference, we have been to France and Turkey; we ski every season, enjoy our friends, and laugh more."

Each morning at Esalen, **Gail Sheehy** could be seen jogging the trails, ponytail flying. Obviously, she hasn't stopped running. Shortly after our dialogue, she published *The Silent Passage*, documenting women's journey through menopause. It maintained its place on the bestseller list for more than two years. In the last chapter, she describes her Esalen experience and quotes from the midlife experiences of several of the participants.

During the 1992 national election campaign, her political profiles in *Vanity Fair* gave millions of Americans a feel for such major players as Hillary Clinton and Dan Quayle. In that year she was voted Best Magazine Writer in America by the *Washington Journalism Review*.

In 1995, Random House published her long awaited sequel to *Passages* and *Pathfinders*. It is *New Passages: Mapping Your Life Across Time*; it defines a new frontier that reflects a recurring theme in our discussions at Esalen: the concept of a second adulthood which opens up at midlife.

We remember well the energy, imagination, and insight she gave to our circle as she began the process of building a framework for this new charting of the life cycle. As she notes in a letter to us, "My indelible experience at Esalen resulted in several vignettes described in the chapter called 'Wisewomen in Training.'" Gail tells us now that she, too, is looking forward to finding a new balance between her professional and personal life. This year she is spending time on the West Coast with her husband, who is teaching a graduate course in journalism at U.C. Berkeley.

Gail contiues to be a close and supportive friend to Group 4; her Foreword to this book epitomizes her enthusiasm in fostering women's networks.

**Mary Louise Smith** has celebrated her eightieth year surrounded, as she writes, by "my clan and 550 of my closest friends." Obviously, this marker has not slowed her pace; her letters brim over with energy. She continues to fly to Washington, D.C., every six weeks for meetings of the U.S. Institute of Peace and is immersed in supporting the Iowa Women's Archives. As she modestly states, "I still keep my hand in politics, of course."

Since the conference, she has faced breast cancer and has become a vocal advocate for early detection. "I was not devastated or demoralized by this experience...but it does make you stop and think." A biography of Mary Louise's life is in the works, "Several years away yet," she reports. "We have been taping over the past two years, researching presidential libraries, gathering it all together." Together, indeed. We would only add, "This is what eighty can and should be like."

The international activities radiating from **Irene Tinker**'s base at the University of California at Berkeley are awesome. If the New Older Woman concept has application beyond our Esalen circle, it is Irene who might take it there. She urges us to remember women of all cultures, from all economic and racial groups, when thinking of future program ideas. During a 1994 sabbatical, she accepted a Residency at the Rockefeller Conference and Study

Center in Bellagio, Italy, and lectured in Norway, Italy, Senegal, Indonesia, and Thailand. Her next major goal is to ensure that women's problems identified in international regional conferences will be adequately addressed at the forthcoming United Nations World Conference for Women in Beijing, in September, 1995. One last predictable word from her: "I did not accept the rich retirement package offered by the University because I have too many projects underway." Irene is a model New Older Woman—using the added gift of time in living each day, week and year fully, happily and productively.

Reporting from Washington, **Harriett Woods** is concluding her term as president of the National Women's Political Caucus, one that put her in the national spotlight almost daily during the '92 and '94 national elections. With the increasing number of women challenging male incumbents, her role as the spokesperson for the leading organization supporting women candidates has been particularly significant. She also chaired the Coalition for Women's Appointments, which has successfully placed a record number of women in senior policy positions in the Clinton administration.

Harriett says: "The Esalen conference came at a very critical juncture for me, just as I was moving from the regional to the national level in Washington, D.C. It is a wonderful reminder of the strength, adaptability, and *endurance* of women through all of the social and personal changes and challenges that we encounter in our lifetimes. The intimate experience with other mature women will be a comfort during the uncertain and very exciting years that are to come."

A few months ago, a San Francisco area paper carried a notice in its *Literary Flash* section: "The public is invited to a reading by **Marilyn Yalom** from her forthcoming book, *A History of the Breast*, preceded by pizza and salad." We were intrigued by the book title, knowing that it was a continuation of Marilyn's life-long study of women as they are portrayed in history and literature (the light menu for the event notwithstanding).

When we spoke with Marilyn recently, she shared a perspective about her work that said something significant about accumulated knowledge. "The last four years could not have been as fruitful for me if I had not been able to call on a store of past experience and past work, which have enabled me to move from a narrow academic world to a broader, wider arena. In writing my book this has been an important aspect—it's a very expanding and satisfying feeling. However, at the same time I'm aware of a closing-off of other kinds of options. I suffered a fracture while skiing this winter, so now I think, 'Well, that's the end of that.'" *A History of the Breast* will be published by Knopf in 1996.

**Gwen Yeo** writes: "I've cut back to 80 percent my work at Stanford Geriatric Education Center because caretaking has become a large part of my life." Her father, mother, and mother-in-law are in institutional care, and, at this point, she is sharing caregiving with her husband. Gwen has contributed one of eight chapters to a *Health Encyclopedia for Older Adults*, to be published in 1996 by Beverly Cracon. In her work at Stanford, she is organizing and participating in several conferences on ethnogeriatrics.

**Eleanor (Ellie) Zuckerman** has, in addition to her practice, been working on reshaping women's consciousness. She operates a study group that is rewriting the old prayers and rituals of Judaism to include women, and she has lectured on the goddess-centered cultures in prehistory, using archeological material recently discovered. Her study also takes a look at the pattern of war culture and how it affects the economy of the world. We never pegged Eleanor as one for small endeavors!

## GROUP 4 AND THE NEW OLDER WOMAN: HERE TO STAY

**Peggy Downes** lost her husband after he battled for five years with cancer; before his death they shared their story in a book, *Dialogue of Hope: Talking Our Way Through Cancer* (Sunflower Inc., 1992), which is used by hospice programs and cancer wellness centers across the country. Their experience is the focus of Chapter Seven—"The Mortality Crisis" in Gail Sheehy's latest book, *The New Passages: Mapping Your Life Across Time.* She is still teaching political science at Santa Clara University and creating interdisciplinary courses interweaving politics, aging, and intergenerational conflict. Last summer, she was a visiting professor at Durham University, England. Peg has begun research for a book, tentatively titled *Going it Alone*, which she hopes will prove helpful to those who suddenly find themselves uncoupled.

As part of **Pat Faul**'s continuing involvement in the worldwide Earthwatch program (an organization that puts volunteers together with research projects), she was part of a 1993 expedition which surveyed the archeological sites along the Turquoise Coast of Turkey. She is working on two writing projects, one fiction and one non-fiction, and has entered the fast lane on the information superhighway with World Wide Web.

The ranch high in the Big Sur mountains that **Virginia Mudd** calls home is still recovering from the worst storms in decades. She's sick of the clean-up, but there's a bright spot: the nearly completed studio at the top of the hill, overlooking a canyon: the room of her own that she's been dreaming of since childhood. Now she must answer the question: "What are you going to *do* there?" First priority is looking at hills, hawks, and horses; then, setting up the workspace, getting acquainted with a woodburning stove and a computer, and thanking her husband. *Then* getting serious about reading all those books and old *New Yorker* magazines she's accumulated all these years.

**Ilene Tuttle**'s eclectic life style has absorbed an array of projects. She continues to organize public cultural exhibitions in what are called "alternative spaces" (outside museum walls), and she consults on special events and exhibition programs for public relations and communications firms. She is writing a book titled *Dear Mr. Lopez*, centering on an exchange of letters between herself as the absentee landlord of a rural southern California property, and her tenant.

As to the four of us, when friends learned we had written a book, the question most asked was, "Are you still friends?" We were certainly vulnerable: four distinct personalities, firm viewpoints, and ways of doing things. We were saved by enthusiasm—in the beginning. A few chapters into the project, seams began to fray; we had to come to terms with our individual styles and work habits. An objective professional intermediary was needed. We consulted the Yellow Pages and found a listing under *Psychotherapy* that read, "Goal Directed Psychotherapy for Individuals, Women's Groups...Conflict Resolution...Stress Management." The therapist met with us for the better part of a day during which we got everything off our heaving chests, cleared the fire from our nostrils, and went home. Weeks passed and we kept writing, having agreed on a division of responsibilities intended to keep us out of each other's hair and egos. And as time passed the pages were completed. To answer the question—we're still friends—friends who are cautious and know where the boundaries are. Are we New Older Women? We like to think so.

As we approach the end of our story, we realize that the doors we opened at Esalen are *still* open to the continuing energy that connected twenty-two very special older American women.

To know we can pick up the phone without advance notice at almost any hour and say simply, "I'd like to know..." or, "Remember when you said...?" or, "Did you ever...?" and we'll be back in instant touch, is a communion of spirit unlike any other we know. We may or may not have portrayed the New Older Woman in a way that has relevance outside this experience, but the term is unmistakably synonymous with the women whose voices we've orchestrated. *They* are the definition.

# Appendix

**RUTH ASAWA**, 69, artist and teacher, San Francisco, was taught by Japanese-American artists from Walt Disney Studios while interned with her family at a relocation camp during World War II. She later studied at Black Mountain college in North Carolina with painter Josef Albers, inventor Buckminster Fuller, and mathematician Max Dehn. She married fellow artist and architect, Albert Lanier and has lived in San Francisco ever since, raising six children. Exhibitions of her sculpture and paintings have appeared at the Museum of Modern Art in San Francisco; the Philbrook Museum, Tulsa; the Oakland Museum of Art; the Whitney Museum, New York; the Fort Worth Museum, and the University of Illinois. Her work is in the collections of the Guggenheim Museum, and the Whitney Museum of American Art, New York; the Addison Gallery, Andover, Massachusetts; the Oakland Museum of Art, Oakland, California. She is the recipient of awards from the Asian Heritage Council, Japanese-American Citizens League, the San Francisco Chamber of Commerce, and the American Institute of Architects. Dedicated to community service and collaborative art, Ruth has received recognition for developing innovative programs with parents, teachers, and children to beautify city schools through art and gardening projects.

**MARY CATHERINE BATESON**, Ph.D., 55, anthropologist, Fairfax, Virginia, is Clarence J. Robinson Professor of Anthropology and English at George Mason University. According to Bill Moyers, she not only studies change—she *lives* it. A Radcliffe graduate, with a doctoral degree from Harvard, Catherine has taught at Amherst, Harvard, Northeastern and Brandeis, as well as universities in Iran and the Philippines. Widely traveled and multilingual, her writings involve sociology, education, linguistics, and psychology. She is author of *Our Own Metaphor* (1972), which deals with consciousness and human adaptation, *With A Daughter's Eye* (1984), a memoir of her parents, anthropologists Gregory Bateson and Margaret Mead, and *Composing a Life* (1989), which re-evaluates feminist agendas in the light of new alternatives, commitments, and transitions. She and her father co-authored *Angels Fear: Towards an Epistemology of the Sacred* (1987). She also co-authored *Thinking AIDS* with Richard Goldsby (Addison-Wesley, 1988), on the social consequences of an epidemic. Her latest book, *Peripheral Visions: Learning Along the Way* (1994), explores the lifelong learning necessary in a rapidly changing, multicultural society. Her honors include a Guggenheim Award, and she is a recipient of the Ford Foundation Fellowship. Currently, she serves as president of the Institute for Intercultural Studies, Inc., which was founded by her mother in 1944, and which is now devoted to preserving the intellectual legacies of Drs. Mead and Bateson. She is married and has a daughter.

**VIRGINIA BOYAK**, Ph.D., 68, industrial gerontologist, Santa Rosa, California, is director of the Human Aging Institute. She is the former director of Aging Studies for Age Wave, an Emeryville, California corporation which provides information on how the aging population affects the marketplace. As a consultant and lecturer, Dr. Boyak travels widely, designing programs for international firms and organizations. Her many clients include Coopers Lybrand, American Express, and American Medical Enterprises. She spoke at the opening session of the 1984 Republican National Convention and was an appointment of Ronald Reagan's Task Force on Long Term Care (1986-88). She also chaired the private sector committee for the White House Conference on Aging (1981). She served as a member of the Business Institute on Aging, Andrus Gerontology Center, University of Southern California, where she was an adjunct professor, and was also the president of the Los Angeles County Commission on Aging. She currently works with Pacific LifeCare Corporation, a non-profit residential program founded by her son. Remarried, with a "his, hers, and ours" family of six children, twenty-five grandchildren, and two great-grandchildren, she is working on a book to be titled *The Option Years* about the dynamics of change in later life. She is an articulate, informed source for older Americans in or facing retirement.

**RUTH BRINKER**, 73, San Francisco Bay Area community activist and civic leader, founded and directed Project Open Hand, which provides services to AIDS victims. A South Dakota farm girl, she attended Northwestern University and the Chicago Art Institute before moving west and marrying. Widowed after eleven years and with two daughters, Ruth began her career writing a pet column for a local newspaper and running an antique shop. She was an early volunteer for Meals on Wheels, which delivers meals to homebound people in the San Francisco Bay Area, and later became a co-director. When, in 1985, she found there was no support system for AIDS sufferers, she conceived Project Open Hand which became a model program nationwide. Executive director for six years, Ruth managed the project as it grew to serve 1,000 meals a day in the Bay Area and had an operating budget of $3.2 million at the time of her retirement. Without taking time for a breather, Ruth focused her energies anew on the plight of the homeless, forming a new organization, Fresh Start Farms, a project that has established a demonstration organic farm to help homeless families become self-sufficient. The Renew America Foundation recently recognized Fresh Start Farms with a Certificate of Environmental Achievement, and a listing in its 1995 Environmental Success Index.

**DENISE SCOTT BROWN**, 63, architect and urban planner, principal in the firm Venturi, Scott Brown and Associates, Philadelphia, was born in Zambia and educated in South Africa and England before emigrating to the United States in 1958. She has taught architecture and city planning as a faculty member of the University of Pennsylvania and the University of California, and has taught at Yale, Oberlin, Harvard, and Rice. Since 1967 she has combined career and family life with her partner-husband, architect Robert Venturi, with whom she has a son. They have collaborated on such major commissions as the Sainsbury Wing of the National Gallery, London, museums in Seattle and San Diego, and the Philadelphia Orchestra Hall. They have co-authored two books, *Learning form Las Vegas* (1972), and *The View from the Campidoglio: Selected Essays 1953–84* (1985). Denise also wrote *Urban Concepts* (1990). She is the recipient of the Chicago Architecture Award; the Order of Merit, Italy (1987); the National Medal of Arts (1993); the 1992 Philadelphia Award; the Benjamin Franklin Medal (1993), and eight honorary degrees.

**LIBBY A. CATER**, 69, consultant and writer, was born and currently lives in Montgomery, Alabama, where she writes and maintains her close contact with and interest in public affairs and women's issues. Her public career began in 1946 when she graduated with honors and a bachelor's degree in economics from the University of Alabama's School of Business Administration. She worked as an administrative assistant for her local congressman, later becoming a research assistant for author Marquis Childs, and for her husband, Washington, D.C., journalist Douglass Cater. When he became a special assistant to the Johnson White House in 1964, Libby worked for Mrs. Johnson on educational and environmental programs. Her career grew to encompass stints as special assistant for Intergovernmental Affairs to Roger Stevens, director of the National Endowment for the Arts; as assistant to the director of the Aspen Institute for Humanistic Studies; and an assistant to Lynda Johnson Robb, chair, President's Advisory Committee for Women. She is co-author of *Women and Men: Changing Roles, Relationships and Perceptions* (1978), published by the Aspen Institute. Active on all fronts, Libby is the mother of four children.

**SYLVIA EARLE**, Ph.D., 59, oceanographic scientist from Oakland, California, who manages careers as research biologist, explorer, environmentalist, and entrepreneur, has had a love affair with the sea since childhood. The world record holder for the deepest untethered ocean dive, her many pioneering accomplishments include her appointment in 1990 as the first female chief scientist of the National Oceanic and Atmospheric Administration (NOAA). Logging 6,000 hours underwater, she has lived for two weeks with four other women in an undersea habitat while cataloging marine life. Her research on environmental damage following the Exxon Valdez oil spill and in the Persian Gulf area, as well as explorations of uncharted underwater territory, have earned her collegial esteem: five species of marine life carry her name. As president and CEO of Deep Ocean Technology , Inc. and Deep Ocean Engineering, her company develops vehicles for ocean exploration, among them Deep Rover, one of the first inexpensive underwater submersibles. Sylvia has taught and been a research fellow at Radcliffe Institute, the Natural History Museum of Los Angeles County, and the Farlow Herbarium at Harvard University, and continues as research biologist and curator at the California Academy of Sciences in San Francisco. She is the author of *Sea Change, A Message of the Oceans* (1995, G. P. Putnam's Sons). The mother of three adult children, Sylvia lives in Oakland, California.

**CLAIRE FALKENSTEIN**, 87, artist, Venice, California, is one of America's major artists, with commissions and exhibitions throughout Europe, the United States, and Japan. She lives and works at her Southern California beach home-studio. Following graduation from the University of California at Berkeley, Claire became an artist and teacher at institutions and museums throughout the West until she moved to Paris in 1950. Sculpture commissions include *Garden Gates*, Guggenheim Foundation, Venice, Italy; *Never Ending Screen*, Grand Canal, Venice; and *Sky Reach*, Phoenix Art Museum. Her drawings are in the collections of the National Museum of Art; the Guggenheim Museum, New York and Venice, Italy; and the Oakland Art Museum. Major exhibitions in France, Germany, and Italy in the 1960s were followed by numerous shows, including those at the Brooklyn Museum, New York; the Boston Museum of Fine Arts; the San Francisco Museum of Modern Art; the Los Angeles County Museum of Art; the Los Angeles Museum of Contemporary Art; the Newport Harbor Art Museum. Claire's art has been the subject of publications and catalogues here and abroad; her selected bibliography includes: *Claire Falkenstein*, Michael Tapie (1958), *General View of Work of Claire Falkenstein*, Ora Leman (1982), *The Continuing Vision of Claire Falkenstein*, a catalogue by Wendy Slatkin (1984), and *Profile: Claire Falkenstein*, by Eleanor Welles. Claire was married for twenty-two years,

but had no children. Now divorced, her former husband
continues to be supportive of her career.

**CECELIA HURWICH**, Ph. D., 75, a research psychologist in
Berkeley, California, is an exemplar of vitality and energy.
Her study, *Vital Women in their 70s and 80s*, earned her a
Ph.D. in Psychology in 1990 from the Center for Psycho-
logical Studies in Albany, California, where she currently
teaches "Issues in Aging." Her work has led to an active ca-
reer in counseling, consulting, and lecturing both in the
United States and abroad. During 1995, she served as a
California delegate to the White House Conference on
Aging, delivered a key address to the American Society on
Aging Conference in Atlanta, Georgia, and chaired a sym-
posium on *Innovative Research for Healthy Aging* at the
First Pan American Congress on Gerontology in Sao Paulo,
Brazil. Cecelia graduated from the University of California,
Berkeley, served as a WAVE in World War II, married, and
raised three children. For eighteen years, she owned her
own interior design firm before developing her current professional interest in aging studies. She is active in women's
advocacy organizations and environmental causes, and her
major recreation, mountain climbing, *began* with a trek on
Mt. Everest at the age of 53.

**SALLY LILIENTHAL**, 75, civic leader, human rights and
peace activist in San Francisco, California, is president and
founder of the Ploughshares Fund, a public grantmaking
foundation dedicated to preventing nuclear war and building global security. Since its founding in 1981, Ploughshares
has made grants totalling more than ten million dollars.
Sally is a member of the Council on Foreign Relations, and
has been a board member of the Center for International
Policy, the Northern California Civil Liberties Union, the
San Francisco Bar Association, and was founder and chair of
the Northern California Committee of the NAACP Legal

Defense and Education Fund from 1971 through 1977. She has had a long association with Amnesty International/USA, serving as Vice Chair for five years, and as coordinator of the Western regional office in San Francisco for seven. In 1990 Sally was honored for her commitment to peace and human rights with the Eleanor Roosevelt Humanitarian Award from the United Nations Association. Other honors include the Robert W. Scrivner Award for outstanding creativity by an individual grantmaker from the Council on Foundations in 1987, an award for Exceptional Commitment to Working for Social Change from the National Organization for Women in 1985, and the Phoebe Hearst Distinguished Woman Award in 1965.

Sally Lilienthal graduated from Sarah Lawrence College in 1940 and is the mother of five children.

**MILDRED MATHIAS**, Ph.D., (1906–95), botanist and emeritus professor of botany at the University of California, Los Angeles, was equally at home in Kew gardens, the jungles of the Amazon, or the campus of UCLA, where she had taught since 1947, and where she was named Emeritus professor of the Year in 1990. She was director of the university's botanical garden from 1968–74, and in 1990, it was named in her honor. Mildred undertook research projects and directed field trips throughout the world, with a special interest in tropical and medicinal plants and natural area conservation. She was a mentor to two generations of scientists and gardeners and the author of numerous articles in scientific publications; six plant species have been named in her honor. In the area of conservation she held numerous offices with the California Nature Conservancy, was appointed a fellow of the California Native Plant Society, and served as chairperson of the University of California's Systemwide Committee for its Natural Reserve System. Her many awards included the *Los Angeles Times* Woman

of the Year, 1964; the Botanical Society of America Merit
Award, 1973; and the American Association of Botanical
Gardens and Arboreta Award of Merit, 1980. Mildred
Mathias died at her home in Los Angeles on February 23,
1995.

**ELIZABETH (BETTE) MULLEN**, 66, is Director of International Activities for the National Association of Retired Persons, Washington, D.C., and was its first director of the
Women's Initiative. She is an honors graduate in Russian
Language and Area Studies at the University of Pennsylvania and has held government positions in Washington and
Germany. Married with two children, Bette and her family
have called Nigeria, Dahomey, Togo, and finally, Belgium,
home. She returned to her alma mater for an M.A. in
African Area Studies, then taught marketing at Wharton
School. She subsequently directed public agencies for community action, development, manpower, and economics in
Philadelphia. In a midlife career move, she entered a computer business in Richmond, Virginia, and, seven years
later, opened the offices of a major California lobbying firm
in Washington, D.C. She has been with AARP since 1982.

**JUDITH PAIGE**, R.D., 57, nutritionist, author, fashion model,
and yoga instructor from Weston, Massachusetts, leads a
multifaceted professional life revolving around her pivotal
interest: healthy living. Her seventeen-year career as a reg-
istered dietitian includes teaching at hospitals, nursing
homes, and prisons. She is a graduate of Simmons College,
and did post-graduate training at Harvard-affiliated hospitals. As the author of *Choice Years: Health, Happiness and
Beauty Through Menopause and Beyond* (1991), she has
been featured on "CBS This Morning," CNN, and the
"Oprah Winfrey Show." Judith also pursues a parallel career as a model with the Ford Models Inc., agency, appear-
ing in nationwide ad campaigns for *Lears*, Clairol, and The

Gap; she has modeled for print ads and feature stories in *Ladies Home Journal, Prevention,* and *Woman's Day* magazines. She is a former yoga instructor at Tufts University and works with private physicians and community groups in her home near Boston. Judith is passing on her healthy outlook to her daughter and new grandson.

**JANE PORCINO,** Ph.D., 71, gerontologist, New York, is author of two best-selling books: *Growing Older, Getting Better* (1983), and *Living Longer, Living Better* (1991), and an assistant professor in the School of Allied Health Professions and director of the Gerontology Program at the State University of New York at Stony Brook. Jane's interest in the health and well-being of women over forty led her to found New York's National Action for Midlife and Older Women, Inc., at Stony Brook, and its publication *Hot Flash,* of which she is editor-in-chief. She is a consultant and writer for such publications as *50 Plus Magazine, Ms, Generations, Perspective on Aging, Mature Outlook, The Gray Panther Manual, The Gerontologist,* and for the National Council on Aging, Washington, D.C. She has appeared on CNN, "EyeWitness News," "HOUR Magazine," and the "David Susskind Show," and on the radio with East Coast Public Radio stations. She has held regional leadership roles with national organizations such as the Gray Panthers, OWL (Older Women's League), and was the founder of Eldershare, a housing group working on Long Island, and the Women's Health Alliance of Long Island. She is a fellow of the Gerontological Society of America and the Brookdale Center on Aging at Hunter College. A full-time mother of six children, she and her retired husband live in New York City.

**JUDY TOWERS REEMTSMA,** 59, Emmy Award-winning television producer, New York, has been associated with a long series of distinguished video programs. She was a researcher-writer for "The Twentieth Century with Walter Cronkite" for CBS News; an associate producer and writer for documentaries with Edwin Newman for NBC News; a producer for the "Magazine" series with Sylvia Chase and Sharon Lovejoy for CBS News; and a producer and senior producer for "CBS Reports," with Walter Cronkite, Bill Moyers ("People Like Us"), and with Marlene Sanders ("Nurse, Where Are You?"). While at CBS News, she produced "Our Times" with Bill Moyers, "The American Parade" with Charles Kuralt, and "Crossroads" with Bill Moyers, before going to PBS where she wrote, directed, and produced "The Health Century," a series done in conjunction with the one-hundredth anniversary of the National Institutes of Health. Winner of three Emmys and the recipient of the George Foster Peabody Award for "In the News," a weekly news series for children, the Albert Lasker Award for "The First Ten Months," and the Columbia Dupont, Writers Guild, and Sidney Hillman Awards, Judy manages her own company, Reemtsma Productions, in New York City. She is married to Keith Reemtsma, M.D., and lives in Manhattan.

**GAIL SHEEHY**, 57, author, New York City, is the author of seven books, including three bestsellers: *Passages*, a landmark work on stages and transitions of adult life; *Pathfinders*, which draws on a study of 60,000 American individuals who transcended life crises, and *The Silent Passage*, a myth-shattering investigation of America's last taboo: menopause. Her latest book, published in 1995, *New Passages: Mapping Your Life Across Time* explores a new frontier: second adulthood. Her other writings explore diverse subjects: healing, hustling, the Black Panthers, and the 1988 Presidential candidates; her most recent is a biographical and psychological portraits of Mikhail Gorbachev and Newt Gingrich. Gail graduated from the University of Vermont and received a fellowship in 1970 to study at Columbia University under her mentor, Margaret Mead. As a journalist, she was an original contributor to *New York Magazine*, and in 1986 became a political columnist for *Vanity Fair*. Gail is a popular lecturer around the country and appears frequently on television news programs. Her honors include the National Magazine Award and the Anisfield-Wolf Book Award; she is a four-time winner of the Newswomen's Club of New York Front Page Award and, in 1991, was voted Best Magazine Writer in America by her peers—readers of the *Washington Journalism Review*. Gail is the mother of two daughters, both published writers, and lives in New York with her husband, publisher and editor, Clay Felker.

**MARY LOUISE SMITH**, 81, Republican party leader, Des Moines, Iowa, served as national chair of the Republican Party in 1974–77, the only woman elected to that post in the party's history. She was vice chair of the United States Commission on Civil Rights in 1982–83 and a Republican National Committee member for Iowa from 1964 to 1984. A member of Iowa's Women's Hall of Fame, Mary Louise has been involved in a wide variety of civic, community, and government affairs in her state and the nation. She has been a trustee of the Robert A. Taft Institute of Government, a founder of the Iowa Peace Institute, a trustee of the Hoover Presidential Library Association, and co-chair of the Des Moines Select Committee on Drug Abuse. She is a founding member of the Iowa Women's Political Caucus and a member of the Advisory Board of the National Women's Political Caucus. She is currently a member of the Board of Directors of the United States Institute of Peace, and derives great satisfaction from her role as co-founder of the Iowa Women's Archives at the University of

Iowa, a project she continues to support and nurture. Mary
Louise is a widow with three children, six grandchildren,
and two great-grandchildren.

**IRENE TINKER**, Ph.D., 68, professor in the departments of
City and Regional Planning, and Women's Studies at the
University of California, Berkeley, has pioneered research
on the impact of development on the lives of women
worldwide. A magna cum laude graduate of Radcliffe with
degrees in political philosophy and comparative government, she received her doctorate from the London School
of Economics on Indian politics; while she was a graduate
student, she drove to India through the Middle East and returned by car from East Africa and back to London with her
husband, whom she had married in New Delhi. Today they
enjoy their three children and three grandchildren. Irene
has always combined scholarship with activism. She
helped found several women's organizations and three research centers: the Wellesley Center for Research on
Women, the International Center for Research on Women,
and the Equity Policy Center, and has represented the
United States in several United Nations bodies. Besides
teaching in the Washington, D.C. area for fifteen years, she
served as the first director of the Office of International
Science at the AAAS (American Association for the
Advancement of Science) and as an assistant director of
ACTION (a volunteer service agency) under President
Carter.

**HARRIETT WOODS**, 68, former president of the National
Women's Political Caucus (1991–95) in Washington, D.C.,
is from St Louis. She was the first woman elected to state-
wide office in Missouri, serving as lieutenant governor
from 1985 to 1989. Previous public service includes: eight
years as a city council member in University City, Missouri;
two years as state transportation commissioner and state

highway commissioner; and eight years as a Missouri state
senator, during which terms she led successful efforts to
strengthen Missouri's drunk-driving laws, to reform nursing-home laws, and to provide more independence for the
elderly and disabled. She also sponsored state legislation
dealing with energy and the environment. From 1989 to
1991, she was distinguished practitioner and president of
the Institute for Policy Leadership at the University of Mis-
souri-St. Louis. In 1982 and 1986, Harriett was Missouri's
Democratic nominee for the U.S. Senate. She attended the
University of Chicago and graduated from the University of
Michigan. She is a former fellow of the Institute of Politics
of the John F. Kennedy School of Government at Harvard
University. Before beginning her public-service career, she
was a journalist, a television moderator, public affairs director, and an independent film producer. Harriett is married to
Jim Woods, a former newspaper editor, and has three sons.
**MARILYN YALOM**, Ph.D., 63, senior fellow and former deputy
director of the Institute for Research on Women and Gender
at Stanford University, was a professor of French at California State University, Hayward (1963–76), and a lecturer in
Stanford's Modern Thought and Literature program
(1976–87). Her course subjects include French and American writers and gender studies. A French linguist, her career as writer, editor, and teacher includes publications in
both English and French. She has authored, edited, or co-
authored nine books, including *Maternity, Mortality, and
the Literature of Madness* (1985), and *Blood Sisters: The
French Revolution in Women's Memory* (1993). In 1992, she
was honored by the French government for her literary accomplishments. Her latest work, *A History of the Breast*,
chronicles cultural ideologies about the breast and the rep-
resentation of it during the past 2,500 years. Marilyn began
her studies at Wellesley College and received degrees in

French at Wellesley, Harvard, and the Sorbonne, with a Ph.D. in Comparative Literature form Johns Hopkins. She has received grants in women's studies from the National Endowment for the Humanities and the National Institute of Education. She taught at Columbia, Johns Hopkins, and the University of Hawaii, and was a professor of foreign languages at California State University, Hayward, before moving to Stanford. Marilyn is married to Irvin Yalom,Professor of Psychiatry at Stanford; they have four children.

**GWEN YEO**, Ph.D., 61, director of the Stanford University Geriatric Education Center, is Senior Research Scholar and Project Director of the Hartford Center of Excellence in Geriatrics at Stanford. She obtained her doctorate from Stanford's School of Education in 1982 in administration and policy analysis research in educational gerontology. She has carried out gerontology research for the National Institute on Aging, the Bureau of Health Professions, the Administration on Aging, and the California Medical Education and Research Foundation. She has chaired the education committees of the American Society on Aging and served on committees of the Gerontological Society of America and the American Geriatrics Society. She was president of the California Council of Gerontology and Geriatrics. Gwen is the author and editor of numerous professional publications in the area of health and aging, and has been the recipient of awards and fellowships from the University of Washington's Northwest Geriatric Education Center, the American Association of Retired Persons, Texas Tech University, and Stanford University's Department of Medicine. She lives in Aptos, California, is married and has two sons and three stepsons.

**ELEANOR ZUCKERMAN**, Ph.D., 62, Clinical Psychologist with a private practice in San Francisco and Orinda, California, is affiliated with the Psychiatry Department of the

California Pacific Medical Center and the San Francisco Psychotherapy Research Group. She has lectured extensively at: the Adelphi University Graduate School of Business Administration, City University of New York, University of California School of Public Health, Stanford University Center for Research on Women, and Mills College, Oakland. A graduate cum laude of Harvard/Radcliffe College, her commitment to women's issues led her to found the Seven Sisters Alumnae Club Presidents' group, the Radcliffe Alumnae Lectureship at Harvard University, and to serve as charter member of the Women's Forum, Inc. Her career has included development of programs in management and career guidance for professional women and the editing of *Women and Men: Roles, Attitudes and Power Relationships*, a compilation of papers from three symposia organized under her leadership. Eleanor has been married for 35 years, and is the mother of two daughters, also graduates of Harvard, who are pursuing careers in investment banking and budget analysis for municipalities.